THE NO SCALES, JUST SONGS VOCAL WORKOUT

VOLUME TWO

A song-based method for warming up
and strengthening the voice

SUSAN ANDERS

Songwriter and Publisher Information

I Can See Clearly Now: ©1972 Johnny Nash • Dovan Music Inc.
I Hope You Dance: ©2000 Mark Sanders & Tia Sellers • Soda Creek Songs/Universal MCA Music Publishing
Bridge Over Troubled Water: ©1969 Paul Simon • Paul Simon Music
Cry: ©2000 Angie Aparo • EMI Blackwood Music Inc
Tracks Of My Tears: ©1965 Warren Moore, Smokey Robinson & Marvin Tarplin • Jobete Music Co
Don't Know Why: ©2002 Jesse Harris • Beanly Songs/Sony/Atv Music Publishing
Why Don't You Do Right?: ©1942 Joe McCoy • Morley Music Co
You Gotta Be: ©1995 Ashley Ingram & Des'ree • Careers-BMG Music Publishing/Sony Music Publishing
You're Still The One: ©1997 Shania Twain & R.J. Lange • Loon Echo Inc/Universal Songs of Polygram
Alison: ©1980 Declan MacManus • BMG Songs Inc
Thank You: ©1997 Paul Herman & Dido • WB Music Corp
Miss Celie's Blues (Sister): ©1985 Quincy Jones, Lionel Richie & Rodney Temperton • Brenda Richie Publishing/Rodsongs/WB Music Corp
Sunday Kind Of Love: ©1946 Barbara Belle, Anita Leonard Nye, Louis Prima & Stanley Rhodes • Universal MCA Music Publishing
Summertime: ©1935 George Gershwin, Ira Gershwin & Dubose Heyward • Dubose & Dorothy Heyward Memorial Fund Publishing/George Gershwin Music/Ira Gershwin Music/WB Music Corp
Dear Prudence: ©1968 John Lennon & Paul McCartney • Sony/Atv Music Publishing
One Of Us: ©1995 Eric Bazilian • Human Boy Music/WB Music Corp
I'm Beginning To See The Light: ©1945 Duke Ellington, Don George, Johnny Hodges & Harry James • Ricki Music Company, Anne-Rachel Music Corporation, Famous Music Corporation
Get Here: ©1988 Brenda Russell • Rutland Road Music/WB Music Corp

Singer's Tools: Tips From the Road ©2003 Susan Anders
reprinted by permission from Backstage West

 Second edition February 2010

Published by Zanna Discs
P.O. Box 58155 Nashville, TN 37205
800-787-2647
www.singersworkout.com • www.zannadiscs.com

Cover by Buckinghorse Design

Table of Contents

Introduction

Several years ago I developed a vocal warm-up that didn't use scales, arpeggios or other exercises. One reason I did this was because I'd worked with many voice students who just hated singing exercises and wanted to get right to singing songs. I'd also watched many other singers master their exercises but still have difficulty applying good voice technique to actual songs. What seemed to work best for them was to start with fairly easy songs that allowed them to focus on technique, then move to harder songs. So I created a sequence of songs that gradually increased in difficulty, and I matched the songs with vocalese sounds that I knew were good for warming up and developing the voice. As the songs progressed, the singer would cover many important aspects of good voice technique, including correct breathing, resonance, range expansion and navigation, diction, and more.

Since releasing the first workout it has been used by singers all over the world with great results, according to the many happy emails I've received. After absorbing the feedback from the first workout and learning some new vocal ideas, I created Volume Two. Singers who have used the first version will be happy to have a set of eighteen new songs to work with, as well as some new troubleshooting tips and technical information. There are chapters on dealing with colds, the environment and aging. I've also included expansion ideas for most of the songs for singers who want ideas on how to stylize the songs once they are mastered. As with Volume One, the type of songs include jazz, r&b, rock, pop, and country.

My thanks go out to the many singers who have given me feedback about the first workout. I'm also indebted to the singers who tested this new set of songs for me, including Darryl Purpose, Julie Zeitlin, Khin-Kyaw Maung, Cecily Gardner, Matt Skinner, Nina Feldman, Tess Skorczewski, Brian Kiernan, Dena Stewart, J.R. Ramos, Lisa Shapiro, and Joyce Woodson. All the voice teachers with whom I've studied over the years have influenced me, but two in particular stand out and deserve special thanks: Lisa Popeil and the late Judy Davis. Thanks as always to my husband Tom Manche, who once again put in triple duty as producer, musician, and copy editor.

How to Use the CDs and Guidebook

The CDs can be used with or without the guidebook to warm up and strengthen your voice. However, I hope that you'll read the guidebook since it's full of useful information, especially if you are a beginning singer. If you want to get right to singing, the CDs alone will work just fine for most singers.

Working with the CDs

Sing along with me (or Perry White if you have the baritone/soprano version) on CD #1 until you learn the melodies and lyrics to all of the songs. Basses will sing an octave lower than my voice, and sopranos will sing an octave higher than Perry. Try the different warm-up sounds I suggest on the CD and see if they work for you—a sound that warms up one voice may do nothing for another, so you will be the ultimate judge. A warmed up voice feels both flexible and strong. You should not feel much sensation in your throat at any time. If you do, you may be wearing your voice out instead of strengthening it. It's fine to repeat songs until they feel right before moving to the next, harder song.

If you are using the workout primarily to warm up your voice before singing other songs, you may use the warm up sounds indefinitely. If you are using the workout to develop your singing ability, you should eventually try singing the song lyrics as well. Beginners especially should work with the warm-up sounds and not the lyrics until they have built up some strength. Beginners may also need to stop after the first few songs the first day, adding songs in the sequence day by day or week by week as their strength increases.

More experienced singers can use the warm-up sounds as they learn the songs or move directly to singing lyrics. Keep in mind that most voices need more warming up in the morning than in the afternoon. If you've had some lessons and know which areas of your voice need the most attention, you can use the songs accordingly, repeating songs or skipping them.

Until you get a feel for the songs, start from the beginning each time you use the CD, unless you use it more than once a day. In that case, you can start where you've left off. If you are using the workout as a supplement to scales and other vocal exercises it's fine to pick and choose the songs you like, but if you don't feel warmed up enough from your other exercises start with the earlier, easier songs. Advanced singers who want to sing the workout in a shorter time period and still get all the way to the last song can try skipping "You're Still the One" and either "Thank You" or "Alison". I'd recommend that beginners go song by song with no skipping.

Once you have the melodies memorized you can use CD #2 and move much faster. On CD #2 the only vocals are mine as I announce the title, the warm-up sound, and the focus for each song. This disc gives you more room for your own interpretation of the songs since it only has music tracks and no melody. Because it has no melody it's also better for working on intonation. At the end of CD #2 you'll find an additional section on how to stylize several of the songs. There you'll find examples of the "expansion ideas" that are in most of the chapters. All of the expansion ideas in the guidebook should be attempted after you are well warmed up and have mastered the song you want to stylize.

If you have trouble singing with just the tracks go back to CD #1 for awhile. Make sure you have the melody down and try counting along with the intros so you know where the vocal comes in.

Singing the first eight to ten songs should be enough to warm up your voice for the day. The second half will help you build more range, strength, volume, and vocal dexterity. Most of these later songs are more difficult. If you feel any vocal strain that isn't relieved by any of the methods cited earlier in the workout, either take a break for half an hour or quit for the day. It's much easier on the voice to work shorter daily sessions as opposed to a long session once a week. Regular daily sessions, even short ones, are also better for building and maintaining vocal strength.

Some of these versions of the songs vary from the original. Long intros and instrumental sections have been edited out so you'll be continuously singing. I didn't always use the key in which the song was originally recorded. Instead, I picked keys that would work for a typical alto and bass or soprano and baritone. Having said that, keep in mind that every voice is different and may not fit perfectly in a typical range. The lowest note altos will sing is the Eb below middle C, the highest is the Eb two octaves above that. Basses will sing the same range an octave lower. The lowest note baritones will sing is the Ab an octave and a half below middle C, the highest is the Ab two octaves above that. Sopranos will sing the same range an octave higher. If a note is too high or low for you to sing comfortably, try the troubleshooting suggestions in the book or find an alternate note. It's never good to force your voice where it doesn't want to go.

Working With the Book and CDs

The guidebook goes deeper than the CDs into many different aspects of voice technique. I discuss a different vocal topic in each chapter, plus I troubleshoot the hard parts of each song. The sequence of topics follows the same general sequence I use when I'm coaching a singer in private lessons.

To get the full benefit of the workout, try this method for using the book and CD together: read the first chapter and try the various sounds before you listen to and sing the first song on the CD. Next, read Chapter Two and do the breathing exercises and postures listed there. Stay aware of your breathing when you sing the second song on the CD. Move through the rest of the book in this same manner, reading about each song before learning it. Repeat songs as much as you like, and move as slowly or quickly as you want. A good pace for a beginner would be to add one song and chapter a week for the first nine songs. The later songs are more advanced, so spend more time with each of them before proceeding.

Another method is to use the guidebook only if you are having difficulty with a specific song. Read the section on that song or go straight to the troubleshooting paragraph. Many singers find it helpful to have the lyrics in front of them while learning a song. Feel free to underline problem words and put in breath marks.

Contemporary vocal styles occasionally bend the rules of good voice technique. A singer may push his/her chest voice too high, or go for a throatier, hoarser, or overly airy tone. You can often get away with these styles if you build up a lot of strength and learn the rules so you can break them intelligently. My recommendation is to strive for great voice technique while singing the workout, even if you plan on bending the rules a bit when you sing your own songs.

I Can See Clearly Now

Focus: Facial Resonance (Placement)
Sound: Humming
Alto/Bass Key: C
Baritone/Soprano Key: F

First, here's a brief anatomical overview of what happens when you sing or speak: As you inhale, your diaphragm (the dome-shaped muscle that essentially bisects your torso) drops and your lungs fill with air. On the exhalation, the air passes through your vocal cords which are actually folds of muscle and tissue right behind your Adam's apple. The air passing through the cords creates vibrations which then resonate anywhere nearby, mostly in your sinus and mouth cavities. You may also feel resonance in your chest or the back of your head or other places, but for now try to focus on the resonance in your sinus and mouth cavity. Here's an important rule of thumb: if you are doing everything correctly, whether singing or speaking, you should feel vibration primarily in your face, not in your throat. I know the vocal cords are in your throat, but you really shouldn't feel that much activity there. Realistically, you should be feeling 95% facial resonance to 5% throat resonance. If you feel a lot going on in your throat as you vocalize you may be heading towards vocal strain. Facial resonance is a sign that you aren't tightening your throat as you sing. It also improves your sound and makes it easier to project.

Another term for facial resonance is "placement." Correct breathing and placement are the two most important facets of good singing. I'll start with placement and then cover breathing in the next chapter. Vocal placement is vitally important for any singer, and even more important for singers with allergies or strained voices.

Try this little resonance test: hum for one second in the middle of your range, neither high nor low. Let the sound fall slightly instead of holding a steady pitch so it's like a quick sigh. You probably feel the sound resonating in your face, somewhere around your mouth, nose or eyes. If not, make sure your hum initiates with a bit of an H, so the sound is "hmmm," not "mmmm." If you still can't feel the buzz, look down at the ground and try again. Tilting is a great quick fix when you've lost facial placement (assuming that you aren't singing while driving!)

Now say "Hmmm-one-two-three" in the same range. When you get to "one-two-three" you should still feel some facial resonance, though probably not as much as with "hmmm." Now count out loud, talk to your cat, whatever, just say anything to see if your speaking voice still resonates in your face.

If this is easy for you, move on. Unfortunately, many singers speak in their throats because of allergies, voice strain, or bad habits. It's the same vocal cords whether you are singing or speaking, singing is just more difficult since one needs to hold a steady pitch. Getting your speaking voice placed right will go a long way towards attaining and keeping vocal strength. It can't hurt to ask yourself a couple of times a day if you feel your speaking voice in your throat or face, especially if you talk a lot throughout the day.

Trying to feel where sound is resonating in your body can seem a bit strange if you haven't tried it before. Some people just don't feel anything at first. If that's the case with you, just hum loose sounds for awhile (like the sounds you made in the first exercise) with your head tilted towards the floor. This should give you a pretty buzzy sound. You can also try touching your face as you hum to feel the vibration. Almost all singers are able to feel facial resonance after a week or two of paying attention.

Feeling sound placement is a key way that singers know they are singing correctly. As your vocal strength grows you will develop a sense memory for how it feels when everything is working right, including placement. Your increased body awareness will give you both greater freedom and more control of your singing.

Warming Up

• Hum the melody at a medium volume. If you don't feel any facial resonance, slowly shake your head "no" as you hum or tilt over from the waist and hum to the floor.

• Sing the lyric. Tilt or slowly shake your head again if you don't feel facial resonance, and sing fairly sloppily, like a drunk jazz singer. This should increase resonance. If you still can't feel any resonance, stick with humming the song.

Troubleshooting

The highest note sung in "I Can See Clearly Now" falls on the syllable "clear," which is a closed vowel—more on these later. If you feel any tension on the high note, drop your jaw a bit and pronounce it so the syllable sounds more like "clih" and not "clee."

Check out versions of "I Can See Clearly Now" by these singers:

Johnny Nash • Jimmy Cliff • Ray Charles

I Can See Clearly Now

Johnny Nash

I can see clearly now
The rain has gone
I can see all obstacles in my way
Gone are the dark clouds that had me blind
It's gonna be a bright, bright, sunshiny day
It's gonna be a bright, bright, sunshiny day

I think I can make it now
The pain is gone
All of the bad feelings have disappeared
Here is the rainbow I've been praying for
It's gonna be a bright, bright, sunshiny day
It's gonna be a bright, bright, sunshiny day

Dear Prudence

Focus: Breathing
Sound: Tongue Rolls and Lip Rolls
Alto/Bass Key: D
Baritone/Soprano Key: F

One of my favorite singers is Vancouver-based jazz singer and teacher Jennifer Scott. She told me a few years ago that she no longer feels the need to warm up her voice, but she does fifteen minutes of breathing exercises daily prior to singing. I do find that I need to warm up my voice daily, but I've noticed that my singing is markedly better after doing an activity that really works my breathing, like yoga or swimming. Need more convincing? Statistically, singers live longer than the average non-singing Joe because we breathe deeper, thus bringing more oxygen to our bodies.

I know that you've been breathing since the doctor slapped your butt when you were born, but good singing requires that you deepen your inhalation and control your exhalation. Life can be stressful and distracting, causing many of us to breathe shallowly. Try a few of the following postures to enhance your respiration. If one doesn't work for you, try another.

Slump over, bending your knees and letting your arms hang like a gorilla. Lift your head slightly only if you feel like you are squishing your throat. Relax your belly as you inhale and you should feel it expanding. This is called stomach breathing or diaphragmatic breathing. The air isn't really going into your stomach; your diaphragm is dropping as you inhale and pushing your stomach out a bit. Slowly stand up straight and see if you can still feel some belly movement on your inhalation. Don't push your stomach out as you inhale, just relax it if you can and let the air fall in.

Put your hands on your waist, thumbs forward. Now lean over at about a 45° angle, straight-backed, with your head up and jaw dropped. Breathe into your hands and feel your lower rib cage expand like a fireplace bellows. This is called "intercostal breathing." This posture is wonderful for increasing lung capacity and encouraging intercostal breathing. Stay in the posture for up to two minutes, breathing deeply throughout. Stand up straight and recover if you hyperventilate and get dizzy. Don't push it. Unless your environment is very humid, do this after you take a shower and the air is moist, and don't do two minutes of this right before a singing session. It's a lot of extra air passing over your vocal cords which could dry them out.

Singers in good physical condition can try a backward bow. Find a couch or easy chair with a padded arm and hang over it, facing the ceiling. Your feet are on the floor, your back just below your shoulder blades is resting on the arm of the sofa, your head is relaxing back, your mouth is open, and your arms are extended above your head. This is a powerful posture that can make your heart pound faster, bringing extra blood to your head and making you dizzy. Please be very careful getting in and out of the posture and don't stay in it for very long. Breathe deeply, feeling your rib cage and stomach expand. This is a great posture for chronic slumpers or shallow breathers.

After fooling around with these postures, stand and breathe deeply again. If you only feel expansion in your upper chest you need to spend more time with the above postures. You may feel expansion in your abdomen, in your lower rib cage, or all the way around your midsection. Voice teachers differ on what is the ideal inhalation. Since you want to stay relaxed as you inhale I don't think you should obsess about the perfect way to do it. As long as you feel expansion somewhere in your belly or lower ribcage you are filling your lungs deeply.

Now for the exhalation. Keep your rib cage lifted as you exhale. Period. Try exhaling on a "ssss," and either watch yourself in a mirror or hold your rib cage to make sure you stay lifted as the air comes out. Pretend there's a string connecting the front of your rib cage and the ceiling (that's what I was told before flunking out of ballet class in third grade, and it works well for singer's posture). Move your head around, walk down the block, do a little dance if you want, but keep that rib cage lifted as the air is coming out. This forces your abdomen and diaphragm to control the release of air. This is what singers call "support."

If you want to go stronger with your exhalation, try adding two more elements. First, keep your rib cage expanded during your exhalation. Some teachers don't like this method, preferring you to think of your rib cage as a fireplace bellows that moves in and out. If that works for you, great. However, I've found that rib expansion on the exhalation increases support. Secondly, keep your upper diaphragm out as you exhale. By upper diaphragm, I mean the area directly under where your rib cage meets in front. You neither want to overly tense nor overly relax this area as you exhale. Think of it as a firm sponge that stays convex while your rib cage stays lifted and you exhale. Watch for throat tension while working this: a tight upper diaphragm can cause a tight throat.

I definitely recommend moving around while you work on your breathing. It will help your inhalation stay relaxed, and keep the rest of your body relaxed as you keep your support muscles firm on the exhalation. Singing is a tricky balance of control and relaxation. If you're tight in the wrong place you can produce a tight, thin sound and develop a sore throat. If you're overly relaxed you can lose your support, run out of air and sing off-key. Finding the right balance of relaxation as you inhale and control as you exhale is critical.

Okay, I'm being long-winded (pun intended). Here's breathing in a nutshell:

- Relax as you inhale, feeling expansion in your belly and/or sides and lower back.
- Keep your rib cage lifted and expanded as you exhale, which forces your lower abdomen and diaphragm to control the release of air.

One final trick: Silently mouth "uh" as you inhale to relax the throat muscles. You may feel your diaphragm drop at the same time.

By the way, breathe through your mouth when singing since it's faster and quieter. Nose breathing is good to do in smoky clubs and as a way to open your sinuses (see Chapter 11 for more about this), but it should be the exception.

Now for some vocalizing. Try a loose tongue roll on "dddd." Keep your rib cage up throughout the exhalation. Though I'm told one can learn to roll the tongue, my experience is that you either can or you can't do it. If you *can* roll your tongue, again make sure that you don't feel much in your throat. "Dddd" is a great initial warm-up sound for sleepy, allergic, fatigued, or post-cold voices. Some singers use it in-between songs to relax the throat when they are working a set of songs.

If you can't roll your tongue, don't despair, you are not alone. Instead, try lip rolls or “motorboating”, which is rolling your lips on a "bbbb" sound. The vibration helps to loosen the area around your mouth.

If tongue and lip rolls are both uncomfortable for you, substitute humming for lip rolls, and quickly say "duh-duh-duh-duh" instead of tongue rolls. All of these sounds are good initial vocalizing sounds and should be fairly easy to place in your face.

Warming Up

• Sing the song using lip rolls, tongue rolls, the sound "duh," or any combination of these three sounds. Concentrate on your breathing.

• Sing the lyric.

Troubleshooting

"Dear Prudence" starts off with very short phrases that have big pauses in-between. Exploit those pauses and use them to take deep, slow, relaxed breaths while maintaining good singing posture: nose straight ahead, rib cage up, shoulders and jaw relaxed. Later in the verse, when the phrases have short pauses, see if you can maintain your deep inhalations, posture and relaxation while inhaling quickly. If you can hear your inhalation you might be tightening your throat. A relaxed inhalation is quiet.

At the end of the fourth line of each verse, on the words "day" and "skies," the melody moves to a low note, then jumps up an interval of a sixth. If that feels too high to do, skip the note and just remain on the low note.

Additional Ideas

Some beginning singers find that there is a big difference between their speaking voices and their singing voices. If your speaking voice feels strong and resonant but your singing voice feels weak on "Dear Prudence," once your breathing feels good try this: during the big pauses that occur in the first half of each verse, right before you sing the second and fourth lines speak "bla-bla-bla" then go right into singing. So the lyric would look like:

(sung) Dear Prudence, (spoken) bla bla bla (sung) won't you come out to play?

The goal is to blur the distinction between speaking and singing so that you sneak the relaxation of your speaking voice into your singing.

Check out versions of "Dear Prudence" by these singers:

The Beatles • Kenny Rankin • Siouxsie and the Banshees

Dear Prudence

John Lennon & Paul McCartney

Dear Prudence
Won't you come out to play?
Dear Prudence
Greet the brand new day
The sun is up, the sky is blue
It's beautiful and so are you
Dear Prudence
Won't you come out to play?

Dear Prudence
Open up your eyes
Dear Prudence
See the sunny skies
The wind is low, the birds will sing
That you are part of everything
Dear Prudence
Won't you open up your eyes?

Why Don't You Do Right?

Focus: Breathing and Placement
Sound: Myah
Alto/Bass Key: C# minor
Baritone/Soprano Key: F# minor

If you forget everything else while you're singing, make your mantra "Breathing and Placement." Those two concepts will carry you a long way towards sounding good and having vocal longevity. Combining them is your goal with this song, but since it's still early in your warm-up I want to also get everything in your "vocal path" loose. The annoying thing about the vocal cords is that they go to sleep when you sleep and have to be gently reawakened daily. Many singers find that they can't take naps before performing without losing their vocal edge. Also, almost all of us carry tension in various parts of our bodies that can affect our voices. Your mouth, jaw, neck, shoulders, and stomach all need to be relaxed to get your best sound.

Some singers go a little wild with the relaxation part of warming up. I know more than one singer who massages her tongue before singing! Some singers don't carry loads of tension in their bodies and go right to singing, while others need 10-20 minutes of body loosening to get a decent sound. Since every singer is different, I'd experiment with a lot of things before singing and see what works for you. Try making faces for face and mouth tension and self-massage for jaw tension. Try not to overly open to stretch out your jaw, I think self-massage where your jaw bones meet is better. Neck rolls and shoulder shrugs help to ease tension in those areas. Sitting in a squat or bending over with your knees bent is good for stomach tension. Swimming and yoga are excellent to do before singing since both encourage stretching and breathing concurrently, just don't wear yourself out. Save some energy for singing, you'll need it. Don't do a bunch of stomach crunches right before singing, since the resulting tight abs could inhibit a relaxed inhalation.

Sloppy sounds are great for initial vocalizing. Yes, you might sound a little drunk or stupid, but your tongue, jaw and throat all relax when you make sloppy sounds. Less restriction on the air flow means more facial resonance, a richer sound, more bang for your buck. You'll also be less apt to grab the notes by tightening your throat as you work through your range. We all want to build vocal strength and control, but at this stage I'd recommend doing anything that gets you and your tension out of the way of your own voice.

What you may not have here is a sense of pitch accuracy. Go for a Billie Holiday feel here and slide on through the sound. Later in the workout when you are well warmed there are several songs that will work that pitch thing. I'm as obsessed with singing in tune as you are, but it's way too easy to overly tighten your throat and face if you worry about pitch accuracy too early in your warm up. Learn from my mistakes: in my early twenties I worked with a teacher who spent a lot of time getting me to loosen my throat. Since I'd developed my pitch control by tightening my throat all the time, I went completely out of tune for a couple of weeks. The players in the band I was fronting at the time were not amused!

If you are convinced that you have serious pitch problems, go ahead and learn the songs without sliding. Instead, sing on "dee" or "da." If you feel any throat tension, slowly shake your head "no" as you sing. Once you feel more solid about the pitch you can gradually go more sloppy or slide-y. Notice how your resonance increases when you do this.

Like tongue rolls from Chapter Two, slow head shaking is another quick fix you can do to release throat tension as you move through the songs. Head shaking is great because you can do it as you sing the lyric.

Though the "ah" vowel and sounds that include it (nah, myah, yah, etc.) are commonly used with beginning singers, some singers have difficulty with it. "Ah" can be hard to control on low notes, and high notes may feel too airy and unresonant. If this is the case with you, try substituting "yeah" for any "ah" sounds that occur in the first half of the workout. "Yeah" is more nasal and therefore more resonant. After a week or two try alternating "yeah" with the "ah" sound. After some time doing this you will probably find that the "ah" sound has become more resonant and can be used on its own.

Warming Up

Check your posture. Imagine a long string attaching the crown of your head to the ceiling, and your body hanging from the string, so your arms and shoulders are relaxed, neither thrown back nor hunched. Your nose should be pointing straight ahead. Keep your rib cage up on both the inhalation and exhalation.

- Loosely sing the melody on "myah" until your throat, face and mouth feel relaxed.
- Switch to singing the lyric.

Continue your sloppy singing when you switch to the lyric to make sure it feels relaxed. You'll probably sound drunk! Gradually use your lips and tongue more crisply to get your enunciation more normal sounding, but go back to drunk singing if you feel any throat tension. Or try sounding drunk, then sober, on alternate lines of the songs. With both methods your ultimate goal is to get clear enunciation as you keep your throat relaxed.

Troubleshooting

If your throat feels tight or your breathing feels restricted when you try normal singing, try the head shaking I mentioned earlier. Or, try swaying your arms as you sing. Just a little bit of movement can do the trick to relax your throat and breathing.

You may notice some notes that feel off or out of tune in "Why Don't You Do Right?" Twice in each verse there is a note that is a little outside of the key. In the first verse those notes fall on "teen" of "Nine-teen," and on "a" of "people make a fool." Those are the correct notes! In blues or blues influenced songs you will often hear notes like these that feel a little dissonant. They're called “blue notes”.

Expansion Ideas

Descending passing tones are a common ornamentation that you can hear in virtually every contemporary style. Try adding one to the last word of the first phrase of "Why Don't You Do Right?" To do that, sing the correct note, then go down the scale two more notes to another chord note. Though they usually pass in stepwise motion down (or up) the scale, sometimes you will skip a note to land on a chord note, like the passing tone on the word "play" in line two of "Dear Prudence." Passing tones done well are both accurate and flowing, so watch that you aren't overly sliding over the notes. Frequently the inflection, that is the note with more volume, is on the first of the three notes. Passing tones will work at the end of every phrase of "Why Don't You Do Right?"

Check out versions of "Why Don't You Do Right?" by these singers:

Ella Fitzgerald • Peggy Lee • Jessica Rabbit

Why Don't You Do Right?

Joe McCoy

You had plenty of money 1922
You let other people make a fool of you
Why don't you do right
Like some other folks do?
Get out of here and get me some money, too

You're sitting down wond'rin what it's all about
If you ain't got no money they will put you out
Why don't you do right
Like some other folks do?
Get out of here and get me some money, too

If you had prepared twenty years ago
You wouldn't be drifting from door to door
Why don't you do right
Like some other folks do?
Get out of here and get me some money, too

Why don't you do right
Like some other folks do?
Like some other folks do?

You Gotta Be

Focus: Relaxing Initial Higher Notes
Sound: Daba or Bada
Alto/Bass Key: Db/E/Eb
Baritone/Soprano Key: Gb/G/Ab

By now, your face and jaw feel loose, your posture is right, your throat feels relaxed, and you can feel facial resonance. Now you can work towards singing higher notes. The majority of singers I've worked with have a harder time loosening up their higher notes than their lows. That's because most of us don't talk like Minnie Mouse all day so those higher notes aren't used until we sing them. In fact, many of us, male and female, talk too low most of the time. It's like we're all trying to sound like cool FM jazz deejays. I'll rail on that subject more in the next chapter.

The most common mistake when singing higher notes is to grab at them. The muscles in your throat tighten and squeeze the vocal cords. The result is a tighter sound, throat tension, and vocal cord fatigue. It's the "squeezing the last bit of tooth-paste out of the tube" school of singing. Some singers do this because they've run out of air, while others just learned to sing with tense throats and have stayed that way.

If your hamstrings are tight and you are trying to touch your toes, you could wrench your back by lurching and straining for the ground. Or, you can gently stretch towards your toes, breathing and relaxing and feeling the muscles gradually loosen. That's how to go for high notes. Gently stretch for them, don't grab. The payoff is vocal longevity and a richer sound.

Tension on high notes can cause singers to go flat. A singer may be fine for almost an entire song, then go for that last high note and be a little under pitch because she's grabbed it. Still not convinced because you've seen some rock singer squeezing out a screaming high note? He probably has had years of lessons and has built up enough vocal strength to get away with all that screaming. Or not: think of all the rockers who screamed through their twenties and had no upper register by their thirties or forties.

As your vocal cords strengthen with practice it will become easier and easier to sing higher notes. But you'll still need to warm up daily. How do you know if you're building strength or overreaching for a note and straining? Again, throat tension and a lack of facial resonance will tell you when you're straining.

Something else to watch for as you initially go for higher notes is what I call "crunching." That's when you furrow your eyebrows together as you reach for high notes. Crunching doesn't look very good, and can lead to facial and throat tension. One of my students got so tired of my comments about her crunching that she had Botox injected between her brows to paralyze the muscle! There are less drastic alternatives. Try raising your eyebrows instead of crunching—this will open your facial and nasal resonators. James Taylor, an awesome singer in my book, raises his eyebrows frequently as he sings. Ronnie Dunn of Brooks & Dunn is another good singer and eyebrow raiser. See the "Thank You" chapter for more on this and the "inner smile."

Singing into the mirror is an easy way to catch yourself if you are a habitual cruncher. Or put a small piece of masking tape between your eyebrows. You'll immediately feel it if you furrow.

Warming Up

• Sing the song on "daba daba" or "bada bada" letting your jaw drop open on the higher notes. "Dabe" works better for most singers on the verse, while "Bada" works better in the chorus.

• Sing the lyric. If any of the higher notes are uncomfortable you can skip them, switch back to "da ba," slowly shaking your head while singing, or go for sloppy enunciation as you did with "Why Don't You Do Right."

Troubleshooting

The way you pronounce some of the words can make them easier to sing. There's more on diction awareness in Chapters 6, 7 and 8, but here are some ideas to get you started:

When you switch from "daba" to the lyric, try not to overly smile as you're singing since this can add tension and cause you to swallow the sound. As a teacher of mine told me years ago, smile through your eyes as you sing, not with your mouth.

The high note of the song is the "my, oh my" right before the second chorus. Drop your jaw to an "ah" shape on "my" to open and relax it.

There are several words ending in R that end phrases in the chorus, including "wiser," "stronger," and "together." Easing up or even dropping the "r" can make those words flow better. Pronounce "-er" like the "ou" in "could," then lightly pronounce the R, if at all. You'll learn more about the consonants R and L in Chapter 8.

Each new verse modulates a half-step higher, so that you are gradually singing higher in your range. Make sure that your voice still feels comfortable as you move to each higher key.

Expansion Ideas

At the ends of phrases try adding a neighboring tone. The first two notes of lower neighboring tones start out just like descending passing tones, but then return to the original note. Upper neighboring tones go to the note above, then return down to the original note. I hear neighboring tones sung fairly quickly these days, but at first sing them slowly (whenever there's room in "You Gotta Be" to sing them slowly) to build accuracy.

Check out the version of "You Gotta Be" by Des'ree.

You Gotta Be

Ashley Ingram & Des'ree

Listen as your day unfolds
Challenge what the future holds
Try and keep your head up to the sky
Lovers, they may cause you tears
Go ahead release your fears
Stand up and be counted
Don't be ashamed to cry
You gotta be

Chorus:

You gotta be bad, you gotta be bold
You gotta be wiser
You gotta be hard, you gotta be tough,
You gotta be stronger
You gotta be cool, you gotta be calm
You gotta stay together
All I know all I know
Love will save the day

Herald what your mother said
Readin' the books your father read
Try to solve the puzzles in your own sweet time
Some may have more cash than you
Others take a different view
my oh my hey, hey

Repeat Chorus

Listen as your day unfolds
Challenge what the future holds
Try and keep your head up to the sky
Lovers, they may cause you tears
Go ahead release your fears
My oh my hey, hey

Repeat Chorus

Summertime

Focus: Low End Placement and Initial Sustenance
Sound: Mee (Mah on highs)
Alto/Bass Key: B minor/Bb minor/A minor
Baritone/Soprano Key: E minor/Eb minor/D minor

You've just focused on keeping your throat relaxed as you ascend to higher notes. At the other end of your range you'll have a different focus. The vocal cords relax as you descend in pitch so throat tension is not much of a problem, but placement and control can be. If the vocal cords over-relax the tone can become too breathy or wobbly, and pitch can be harder to control. It may feel like the sound is in your throat. That's a weird phenomenon: both over-relaxing your low notes and straining on your high notes can feel throaty.

Your goal on low notes is to continue feeling facial placement. On your lowest notes you should still feel some facial "buzz" though you won't have much volume. That's how the voice works, so don't bother trying to increase the volume of your voice on your low end, you'll just strain it.

Trying to force your voice to go lower can tire you as much as forcing high notes. This counts for talking as well. Most speech therapists think that the average person speaks too low, causing strain. If you find that your voice gets tired from talking but not from singing, you may be speaking too low. When singing, if you think you are bottoming out on a low note, try humming it or singing it on "mee." If you still feel the note in your throat, substitute a higher note for the day and try again tomorrow.

Many singers find that their voices naturally rise in pitch as the day progresses. That means lower notes will be easier to sing early in the day, and higher notes will be easier in the evening. I once recorded a song where I wanted to use my very lowest notes. Since vocal cords are very relaxed when we first awaken, I went to the recording studio first thing in the morning and didn't speak or vocalize at all before recording the song. That dropped me from an alto to a tenor.

Try to sing with no vibrato when you are initially warming up your low notes. That will cause your vocal cords to hold a bit more firmly, which will strengthen them and give you better facial placement. A little bit of a smile can help control low notes, too. Yes, in the previous chapter I talked about not overly smiling when singing, but make an exception for low notes.

You'll also be doing some initial sustenance work with this song. Sustenance calls for good breath control and some vocal strength. If either is lacking you'll feel the sound in your throat. If slowly shaking your head on any sustained note doesn't relieve the strain, you may have reached your sustenance limit for the day. Back off and shorten how long you hold the note, and don't worry. Just by singing these songs over time your ability to sustain notes will increase. Review the "sss" exercise in Chapter 2 to focus on breath control.

Warming Up

• On all the high notes of "Summertime" sing "mah," and on all the low notes where you want more control sing "mee." Here's where the "mahs" and "mees" fall:

mah mah mah mah mah mah mah mah mee mee
Sum-mer-time and the li- vin' is ea-sy

mah mah mah mah mah mah mah mah mah mah
Fish are jum- pin' and the cot-ton is high

mah mah mah mah mah mah mah mah mah mee mee
Your dad-dy's rich and your ma-ma's good loo- kin'

mee mee mee mee mee mee mah mah mah
So hush lit- tle ba- by, don't you cry

Drop your jaw on "mah" and close your mouth so there is no space between your upper and lower teeth on "mee." If you prefer you can substitute "la" and "lee." If you lose your placement on the low notes, hum them instead for a week or more.

• Switch to the lyric. You will probably lose a bit of resonance with this switch, but if you can't feel any resonance at all on the low notes you can substitute "mee" for words for awhile. Or try tilting your head down slightly and smiling as you sing the low notes.

Troubleshooting

Finding the right mouth position will make sustaining the long notes much easier. There is a detailed discussion of diction in the next three chapters. Try the following mouth shapes for these held notes:
"Ah" with a dropped jaw on the "time" of "Summertime."
"Eh" (or in-between "ih" and "eh" if you prefer, with a halfway-dropped jaw for the "in" of "jumpin'." Do the same for "rich," and the "in" of "mornin.'"

Again, if using the correct mouth shape and/or slow head shaking doesn't eliminate throat tension on the sustained notes, cut them short for now.

Regardless of the vowel, close your mouth back up for the low notes. Many of the low notes in "Summertime" fall on easier to control closed vowels, which is why I picked the song.

"Summertime" modulates down each verse so that you are gradually working lower and lower. If despite smiling, tilting over, closing your mouth more, and using "mee" you still feel the lowest notes in your throat, you may have reached the low end of your voice for now. Skip those notes. You can avoid the lowest note by staying on the same note for both syllables of "easy" in the first line, then following suit on later lines. Depending on the shape and size of your vocal cords, you may or may not be able to increase the low end of your voice. Frankly, it's usually easier to increase the upper end of one's register. If you are a teenager, be patient. Your voice will continue to deepen into your twenties. If you are any age and carry a lot of tension in your throat, your range will increase at both the low and high ends as you learn to vocalize without throat strain.

Expansion Ideas

Since "You Gotta Be" is pretty fast, try some more neighboring tones on the first lines of "Summertime" to make sure you've got them. Then try some ascending passing tones. These work the same way as descending passing tones: sing the correct note of the melody, then rise up the scale two notes. That last note should also feel like it works with the accompaniment. Ascending passing tones aren't used as frequently as descending ones in most contemporary styles, but they are a nice occasional touch.

You can also sing a descending passing tone if you don't want to stay on any of the sustained high notes. If you listen to other singers you'll hear that many of the fills and runs they do are to get out of singing a difficult note!

Check out versions of "Summertime" by these singers:

Sarah Vaughn • Janis Joplin • Sam Cooke • Ella Fitzgerald

Summertime

George Gershwin, Ira Gershwin & Dubose Heyward

Summertime, and the living is easy
Fish are jumpin', and the cotton is high
Your daddy's rich, and your mama's good lookin'
So hush little baby, don't you cry

One of these mornin's
You're gonna rise up singin'
Then you'll spread your wings
And take to the sky
But till that mornin'
Ain't nothin' can harm you
With daddy and mama
Standin' by

Summertime, and the living is easy
Fish are jumpin', and the cotton is high
Your daddy's rich, and your mama's good lookin'
So hush little baby, don't you cry

One Of Us

Focus: Simple Vowels
Sound: Yeah (Yah on Chorus)
Alto/Bass Key: G/Ab/A
Baritone/Soprano Key: D/Eb/E

You may have noticed while singing the last few songs that some vowels feel better to you than others. Common vowels that are easier to sing include "ah" and "oh" on high notes, and "ee" and "oo" on low notes. That's because low notes are easier to control on words with closed vowels like "ee," while high notes are easier to stay relaxed on with open vowels like "ah." When I say closed or open I mean what your jaw must do to pronounce the vowel. Knowing a bit about vowels and diction can make singing easier. You don't need to analyze every single word you sing, though I did just that with a couple of my teachers. Studying diction can train your mouth to pronounce each word in the easiest way possible. After awhile it becomes automatic. Remember, we can't tell our vocal cords what to do, but we do have some control over our mouths, tongues and soft palates (more on your soft palate in Chapter 11). How you pronounce each word can improve your sound and maximize the ease with which you sing.

What you're learning here is a "singer's diction" that is slightly different than the way we speak. You may have noticed many singers, like Paul McCartney, Faith Hill, or Celine Dion, speak with an accent that is distinctive to the region where they grew up, but have no accent when they sing. They all are using singer's diction. For some styles of singing you may want to have an accent to sound authentic: bluegrass singers have a southern twang, British punk singers keep their english accents, and blues singers have a more soulful, relaxed diction. Singer's diction still works for all of these as long as you know how to bend the rules to fit your style. Some country singers, for example, close their mouths more than normal while singing to get a nasal twang, then sacrifice the twang and open wide only on difficult high notes.

Another reason to study singer's diction is that it trains your tongue. Remember, we can't get at the vocal cords, but we have control over our tongues (though it doesn't always feel that way!), and what the tongue does influences the vocal cords. Just as you want your singing to be a balance of relaxation and control, as you vocalize a vowel your tongue should be relaxed, but firm. The tip should be right behind your lower teeth, touching them, and the sides of your tongue should rest against and slightly on your lower molars. If you never had to pronounce a consonant, this is the position your tongue would stay in as you sing different simple vowels. Of course, once you are pronouncing real words your tongue will release from this position to articulate the consonants, but this is where it should be whenever you sustain a vowel.

You may find that you are using your jaw muscles more as you try to not overwork your tongue. This is normal, but you might want to massage your jaw periodically during singing practice so tension doesn't build up.

Good singer's diction is invisible, and because it uses the easiest pronunciation of each vowel sound it frees and opens up your sound. You shouldn't sound "trained" after you've worked on diction for awhile, though if this work is new to you it may take awhile to feel and sound natural. Even if you want to retain a distinct accent when you sing, it helps to study diction so you can use it to troubleshoot difficult notes.

Your voice projects out of you on vowels. Almost all consonants stop the sound and cannot be sustained. While consonants are very important, for now focus on finding the vowel sound in every word you sing.

Simple vowels are vowels like "ah" and "ee" that come from one jaw and lip position: drop your jaw and make a sound and it's "ah." Bring your lips forward from there like a fish and you get "aw." Here are all of the simple vowels:

Vowel	Jaw Position	Lips Position
ee (see)	closed	slight smile
oo (too)	closed	forward
ih (this)	closed	relaxed
eh (bet)	halfway open	slight smile
ou (book)	halfway open	forward
uh (dud)	halfway open	relaxed
a (cat)	halfway open	smiled
ah (hot)	fully open	slight smile
aw (lawn)	fully open	forward

On slight smile vowels you should look interested, not grinning. On forward vowels your lips, especially your upper lip, should stay soft, as if you were kissing someone. Many singers find simple vowels to be pretty easy to deal with because they aren't that different from how we speak, but some have tense speaking habits that they carry into their singing. The most common problems I see are singers that don't open their mouths enough on halfway and fully open vowels, and singers that overly smile or "pull" their vowels. Halfway open is about the width of your thumb, and fully open is about the width of your index and middle finger held together. You can adjust your jaw a bit depending on the note. Close up a bit for lower notes, open more for higher notes.

If you are pulling some of your vowels, try singing into the mirror. You'll immediately see which vowels are troublemakers for you. Try to replace the horizontal increased smile with a vertical jaw drop and notice how it feels easier and looks more relaxed. Another way to monitor is to place three fingers on the hinge of your jaw as you sing to make sure you aren't grinning too much.

Warming Up

• You've already sung some sounds with simple vowels in the workout: "mee," "mah," and "myah." "Yeah" is a halfway open sound that should be easy to use on the lower verses of "One of Us." You can also use "yeh" (eh as in bread) if you prefer. "Yeh" is slightly more relaxed than "yeah," and both of them are halfway open sounds with simple vowels. You can alternate them if you like. If neither "yeah" nor "yeh" are comfortable for you at first, substitute "yah." You can also sing "yah" only on the choruses if "yeah" feels tight on them.

• Sing the lyric. To increase your diction awareness, notice how your mouth is shaping some of the simple vowels. This will be easier on the chorus, which has fewer lyrics. Here is the chorus with some of the sustained simple vowels underlined. "God" and "slob" have "ah" vowels while "us" and "bus" have the "uh" vowel.

What if God was one of us?
Just a slob like one of us?
Just a stranger on a bus
Trying to make his way home

The first line of the chorus has words that include all simple vowels. Try singing that line very slowly to feel how you are shaping each vowel.

Troubleshooting

The highest notes fall on the words "God," "slob," and "stran-" of "stan-ger" on the chorus. "God" and "slob" both have "ah" vowels, so drop your jaw to open them. If they are hard to sustain at first, dive off of them towards the lower notes. As they get stronger try to hold the pitch until you move to the next note. On "stran-" shape and sustain the vowel "eh," only articulating the "n" right before you move to the lower note for "-ger." As always, you can slowly shake your head to keep your throat relaxed as you moved to higher notes, like when the final chorus modulates a half-step higher.

Don't be taken by surprise as the pre-chorus moves into the chorus. There is so much room to breathe during all the "Yeah yeah yeahs" that you could get a false sense of security. Then when the melody suddenly links three "yeahs" to "What if God was one of us" you could run out of air. Make sure your breath before those final three "yeahs" is a good one.

Expansion Ideas

When songs are wordy like "One of Us" there isn't a lot of room for fancy fills. What *would* work here is the appoggiatura, a deceptively simple ornament heard in all popular styles. An appoggiatura is like an upper neighboring tone where you skip the first note. That means you jump directly to the note above the melody note, then resolve down to it. Try this on the first line on the word "name." With passing tones and neighboring tones you start with the correct note and then move away. What's difficult about singing an appoggiatura is that you are jumping right to a non-melody note that often is slightly dissonant to the chord being played. I love the subtlety of appoggiaturas and think they are worth the effort to master.

Check out versions of One of Us by these singers:

Joan Osborne • Seal

One Of Us

Eric Bazilian

If God had a name what would it be
And would you call it to his face
If you were faced with him in all his glory
What would you ask if you had just one question
Yeah, yeah, God is great
Yeah, yeah, God is good
Yeah, yeah, yeah yeah yeah

What if God was one of us?
Just a slob like one of us?
Just a stranger on a bus
Trying to make his way home?

If God had a face what would it look like
And would you want to see
If seeing meant that you would have to believe
In things like heaven and in Jesus and the saints
And all the prophets, and
Yeah, yeah, God is great
Yeah, yeah, God is good
Yeah, yeah, yeah yeah yeah

What if God was one of us?
Just a slob like one of us?
Just a stranger on a bus
Trying to make his way home?

Get Here

Focus: Working with Diphthongs
Sound: Why, Way
Alto/Bass Key: Bb
Baritone/Soprano Key: Eb

As I mentioned last chapter, simple vowels are pretty easy to handle once you understand them. It's diphthong vowels that are the troublemakers when singing. Diphthong vowels are a combination of two vowel sounds, an open vowel followed by a closed one. When you slowly say the word "why," for example, you'll notice that your mouth moves to complete the vowel sound, shifting from an "ah" shape to an "ee" shape. If you try to pronounce a diphthong without moving from the open to the closed vowel it tends to feel swallowed and throaty. Breaking the diphthong into its two simple vowels makes it easier to sing. Since high notes are easier to sing on open vowels, focusing on the open half of the diphthong makes high notes easier to reach and sustain.

After working with diphthongs for awhile your mouth remembers what to do automatically. You sing "why" and your mouth moves to an "ah" shape, the first half of the long I diphthong.

Here are the diphthongs English-speaking singers use:

Diphthong	As in		Open Vowel		Closed Vowel
long I	why	=	ah	+	ee
Ow	wow	=	ah	+	oo
long A	way	=	eh	+	ee
long O	no	=	aw	+	oo
Oy	boy	=	aw	+	ee

The most important part of working with diphthongs is knowing what the open vowel is for each one. As you finish the word your mouth will naturally go to the closed vowel.

How you pronounce your diphthongs will help you tweak your singers diction to fit the style of music you sing. Here are some of the ways to use diphthongs to make the word "why" fit different styles:

Why="W" + "ah" + "ee"
Country and bluegrass: close in quickly to the "ee"
Show tunes: deliberately pronounce both the "ah" and "ee"
Jazz: pronounce both "ah" and "ee" but fluidly move from one to the other
Pop: spend most of your time on the "ah," just touch on the "ee"
Rock and R&B: spend most of your time on the "ah," then close to a relaxed "ee," more like an "ih"
Blues: spend most of your time on the "ah," then barely pronounce the "ee" or drop it

completely.

Listen to some of your favorite singers when they are sustaining a word with a diphthong and see how they handle it.

Warming Up

• Sing "Get Here" using "why" (long I diphthong) on the first verse and "way" (long A diphthong) on the second verse, then alternating from there. You can do one "way" per note, but my preference is to do two notes for each "way" or "why." On "why" dwell on the "ah" vowel, on "way" shape the "eh" vowel. See the simple vowel chart in the previous chapter if you need exact mouth positions for either. You can also alternate singing "why" or "way" every other day instead of every other verse if you like.

• Sing the lyric. The lyric includes many words that have long I or long A diphthongs, like "rail-way," "trail-way," "plane," and "mind," so you'll have prepared for them by practicing with "why" and "way."

Since "why" has the more open vowel "ah" in it, use it when you get to the higher notes that occur during the bridge.

Troubleshooting

The highest notes are in the bridge; "my" of "had my way," and "I" of "I need you closer." Both have long-I diphthongs, so go for the "ah" and open up, especially during the quick jump to the high note on "my."

If you find you are "pulling" or overly smiling the diphthongs, either sing into a mirror or rest your hands on either side of your mouth as you sing. Continue to work towards a vertical mouth opening instead of a horizontal one.

Because the chords and melody are a bit jazzy, some of my students have had a hard time tuning "Get Here." If this is the case with you, spend a fair amount of time singing the melody with me while you listen to the band, especially the keyboard, so you can hear how they work together.

Expansion Ideas

Can you hear the appoggiaturas that are written into the melody of "Get Here"? There's one on the word "mind" at the end of the fourth line. You can add a fill to one that already exists in the melody to create combination fills. A common one is a neighboring tone that falls in the middle of an appoggiatura—it sounds complicated but you'll hear that it isn't when you listen to my recorded example on CD #2. "Mind" is sung over a two note appoggiatura: sing the first note, add an upper neighboring tone, then resolve down to the second note of "mind."

Check out versions of "Get Here" by these singers:

Brenda Russell • Oleta Adams

Get Here

Brenda Russell

You can reach me by railway
You can reach me by trailway
You can reach me on an airplane
You can reach me with your mind
You can reach me by caravan
Cross the desert like an Arab man
I don't care how you get here, just
Get here if you can

You can reach me by sailboat
Climb a tree and swing rope to rope
Take a sled and slide down the slope
Into these arms of mine
You can jump on a speedy colt
Cross the border in a blaze of hope
I don't care how you get here, just
Get here if you can

There are hills and mountains between us
Always something to get over
If I had my way, surely you would be closer
I need you closer

You can windsurf into my life
Take me up on a carpet ride
You can make it in a big balloon
But you better make it soon
You can reach me by caravan
Cross the desert like an Arab man
I don't care how you get here, just
Get here if you can
I don't care how you get here, just
Get here if you can

I'm Beginning To See the Light

Focus: Diphthongs, Looping, R & L
Sound: Wo, Wow
Alto/Bass Key: D
Baritone/Soprano Key: G

There are two big differences between singing and speaking. When we sing we hit specific notes and we sustain them. You hold a note on the vowel sound, not the consonant. As I mentioned before, most consonants can't be sustained. Try sustaining P, D, or T, and you'll prove it cannot be done. Your vocal sound projects out on vowel sounds which is one reason we've been spending some time on simple vowels and diphthongs. Articulating consonants is important, too, of course: articulation is discussed in Chapter 15.

There are six consonants that can be sustained: R, L, M, N, S and Z. Of these, R and L are the most problematic. If you overly sustain any of the others it sounds funny and you'll automatically stop. Many of us emphasize R and L when we speak and then carry that into our singing. Like diphthongs that are mispronounced, this can cause a swallowed or twangy sound.

Here's a weird thing about R and L: they only tend to be swallowed when they occur at the end of a word. Slowly say "red car." For most people the R of "red" will feel like it's articulated in the front of the mouth, while the R of "car" will sit at the back of the tongue. Notice the same thing with "Late call."

How much you want to sustain any Rs or Ls that occur in a word is ultimately your artistic choice. If you listen to different singers you'll hear a lot of variation in their articulation of R and L (especially R) that, like diphthong pronunciation, contributes to their distinctive style. Though there is a lot of variation within each style, in general:

Traditional Country/Bluegrass—strong R/L: Patty Loveless, Alan Jackson
Show tunes—distinct R/L: Audra MacDonald, Michael Crawford
Jazz—distinct to very light R/L: Ella Fitzgerald, Natalie Cole, Harry Connick Jr., Louis Armstrong, Norah Jones
Pop or Country/Pop—light R/L: Dido, James Taylor, Martina McBride
Rock—light to nonexistent R/L: Steven Tyler, Melissa Etheridge, Sheryl Crow
R&B or Pop/R&B—light to nonexistent R/L: Beyonce, Celine Dion, Justin Timberlake
Blues—nonexistent R/L: BB King, Etta James

One way to spend more time on a vowel and de-emphasize R and L is to "loop" your words together. Looping is when you connect the end consonant or consonants in a word or syllable over to the next word or syllable. Here's a line from "I'm Beginning To See the Light":

But now that the stars are in your eyes

Here's what it looks like if you loop the words:

Buh tnow theh tthe stah rsaw rih nyaw reyes

Notice how with looping, the R that falls at the end of "stars" and "your" now starts the next word and is pronounced more in the front of your mouth. It looks and sounds funny to speak it like this but try singing these words over the melody and you'll hear how looping can open up your sound.

You can go too far with looping and singer's diction, of course. You may feel like a robot for awhile as you sound some of these words out and explore the most open way to pronounce each one. Outside of show tunes, you ultimately don't want your diction to sound overly trained. Awareness of simple and diphthong vowels, Rs, Ls and looping are all elements to make you sound more free and natural.

Warming Up

- On alternate verses of "I'm Beginning To See the Light" sing "wo" or "wow." On the "wo" diphthong your mouth should shape an "aw" vowel, while on the 'wow" diphthong you'll be shaping an "ah." Since the notes move by fairly quickly you may only be aware of your mouth shape on a few of the notes. If you want more time on each "wo" or "wow" do one for every two notes.

- Optional: occasionally substitute the sound "woy" (rhymes with boy) at the end of a phrase or for an entire phrase. In real life you won't come across the "oy" diphthong as frequently as other vowels, but you might as well prepare for words like "joy" and "noise." If it's too complicated to remember this, stick with "wo" or "wow."

- Sing the lyric, looping the words.

Troubleshooting

The first high note falls on the word "eyes" in the third phrase. Dropping your jaw into an "ah" shape will make it easier to sing, as will looping the R from "your" over to "eyes." Focus on an "aw" mouth shape when you encounter that high note again on the word "low" in the next verse. Think "ah" again on "fire" at the end of the bridge, and again on "mine" in the last verse. All the highest notes in "I'm Beginning To See the Light" are on diphthongs, so emphasizing the first open vowel of the diphthong will free up those words.

It helps when learning the melody on the bridge (starting with "Used to ramble through the park") to know that the first three phrases share the same melodic shape. Each phrase is a half-step lower than the previous phrase.

There isn't a lot of breathing room in the verses, just one beat at the end of each phrase. Don't sustain those phrases or you'll cut into your breathing time. All it takes to inhale faster correctly is concentration. There's no change in how you inhale, you'll just be doing it more quickly. Try putting your hands at your waist or belly to make sure that you are breathing deeply. Focus on relaxing your throat on the inhalation, watch for gasping, and you will eventually get a full, relaxed inhalation in just one beat.

Expansion Ideas

Because it moves at a steady pace, there isn't a lot of room for ornamentations in "I'm Beginning To See the Light." However, since it's a jazz standard it's a great one for working on phrasing. Phrasing is when you keep the same notes but play around with the rhythm. You may not hear a lot of phrasing done on pop, rock or country songs that are tied to the beat, but listen to jazz, blues and rap and you'll hear a lot of it.

The first step with phrasing is to get used to *not* singing with the beat. This is easy for some singers, harder for others. You're going to try the "straightening out the swing" method here. If it's hard to get a handle on, skip it for now. Instead, learn about and try "back-phrasing" with "Sunday Kind Of Love" when you get to Chapter 10. Then come back to this one.

"I'm Beginning To See the Light," "Sunday Kind Of Love," and "Why Don't You Do Right?" are all swing songs. They have a bouncy or galloping feel. For those of you who know your time signatures, it's like a 12/8 song where the first two of every three eighth notes are tied together. In contrast, "I Can See Clearly Now," "One of Us," and "Don't Know Why" are all straight feel songs. To get used to phrasing with "I'm Beginning To See the Light," try singing the notes straight instead of swinging them. This is a hard one to describe in words, the easiest thing to do is to listen and copy my example at the end of CD #2. I've heard jazz singers do straight against swing phrasing through entire songs, or just on a phrase or two during the song. At first it may feel like you're trying to rub your tummy and pat your head concurrently. One way to get used to singing a rhythm that doesn't lock into the accompaniment but plays against it is to tap your hand or feet to the beat as you sing.

Check out versions of "I'm Beginning To See the Light" by these singers:

Rosemary Clooney • Natalie Cole • Frank Sinatra • Bob Dorough

I'm Beginning To See The Light

Duke Ellington, Don George, Johnny Hodges & Harry James

I never cared much for moonlit skies
I never wink back at fireflies
But now that the stars are in your eyes
I'm beginning to see the light

I never went in for afterglow
Or candlelight on the mistletoe
But now when you turn the lamp down low
I'm beginning to see the light

Used to ramble through the park
Shadow boxing in the dark
Then you came and caused a spark
That's a four-alarm fire now

I never made love by lantern shine
I never saw rainbows in my wine
But now that your lips are burning mine
I'm beginning to see the light

Don't Know Why

Focus: Register Navigation, Vibrato
Sound: Yah
Alto/Bass Key: Bb
Baritone/Soprano Key: Eb

You may have noticed as you've sung some of the higher notes in the workout songs so far that your voice shifts or changes quality at certain spots. The vocal cords are making adjustments as you move from note to note, and in some places within your range you may really notice an obvious adjustment. Your voice may sound lighter and airier, and you may notice some bumps or breaks as the sound shifts. Or, you may have felt that you hit a wall on some higher notes that your voice can't pass. That means you are stuck in one register of your voice and can't get to another.

Some voice teachers don't like to talk about the different registers of the voice since the ultimate goal is a seamless voice from high to low, but I think it helps to know what you're doing. Also, some styles of music actually use the break in the voice as it moves to an upper register. I think that singers should have as large a vocal palette as possible, and understanding vocal registers will increase your palette.

Most of us speak in what is called the chest register. Since we tend to speak at the low end of our vocal range, the lower notes we sing are also in chest register. Many singers only sing in their chest register, and a great deal of what you hear when you turn on the radio is chest register singing. Country, blues, rock, and belted show tunes use a lot of chest voice. Most of the workout songs up to now fall into a typical chest register range, though some of the altos and sopranos may also be using their head registers on the high notes.

There is a limit to how high one can sing in chest register, so to expand your range you either have to increase your chest register (which can be done to a limited extent), or move into other registers. Forcing your chest voice too high is one of the most punishing things you can do to your vocal cords. If you find yourself pushing or yelling the high notes during the workout you should pull back on your volume. This will encourage your voice to shift to a higher register. Chapter 18 addresses how to safely "belt," or carry your chest voice to higher notes.

As one vocalizes higher notes, the vocal cords reach a point where they can no longer produce the sound in chest voice. Many voices at this point will suddenly shift into a head voice. Male singers often call the head voice the falsetto. It feels and sounds lighter, sometimes airier, and resonates more in the head. Classical sopranos, traditional female folk singers, and some r&b tenors use a lot of head voice. Some sopranos use a lot of head voice in contemporary singing, and some beginning female singers and some pre-puberty children of either gender sing completely in head register. Don't force your voice into chest register if it isn't ready to go there, you'll only strain your voice. If you are past puberty and think that you are stuck in your head voice on lower notes and you see no improvement after using the workout for a month, a visit to a voice teacher may be in order. It shouldn't take long to release your chest voice, but it's best if a professional can monitor you during the process.

Some singers, like Hank Williams and Dido, use the break between registers for an effect: Hank Williams yodels through the first line of "Lovesick Blues," and Dido lets her voice break in a lovely way on the chorus of "Thank You." Other singers, like Marvin Gaye, Al Green, early Joni Mitchell, Jeff Buckley, and Eva Cassidy, smoothly swoop from head to chest register without a bump.

Even if you want to let your voice break occasionally, I still recommend that you warm up in a very fluid style that smooths out any register bumps. It's pretty easy to let your voice break if you want it to, but much more difficult to get it moving freely from register to register. There are several transitional bridges in the voice to navigate across as you sing through your entire range. Regardless of the register you are in, you should still feel facial resonance and your throat should be relaxed.

There is a also a middle register in-between the chest and head voice called the mix that I'll discuss in the next chapter. If you notice as you sing that your voice is resonating somewhere that doesn't feel like a chest or a head voice, you're probably in your mix register—that's a good thing!

"Yah" is a great sound for smoothing out register bumps and singing higher notes without straining. The Y helps to focus the sound so it isn't too airy, and the "ah" vowel causes the jaw to drop and the throat to open. This makes high notes easier to reach and helps you slide through the transitional passages of the voice. If "yah" is at all difficult for you, try substituting "nah."

With good singer's posture and breathing, sing a long extended "yah" yawn-sigh that swoops from comfortably high to comfortably low. Try to start on a note in your head voice. Because "Yah" has an open vowel in it you may not feel loads of facial resonance, but you shouldn't feel much of anything in your throat. Keep your tongue relaxed and try not to let it retract from its normal place. See Chapter 6 if you want to review tongue placement.

If you have never sung in head voice you may experience a lot of bumps as you initially wake up these higher notes and blend them into your lower register. You might want to try tilting over as you sing to bring out more head resonance, or try slowly shaking "no" as you sing to release throat tension. Be patient with yourself if this is a new area of your voice, and keep in mind that it's new territory— your muscles need time to become more elastic.

The majority of singers I've taught find it easier to sing higher notes by starting on the note and swooping down, but some singers find it easier to swoop up to high notes from below. There's no right nor wrong with this, just what's easier for you. If you fall in the latter group, do some backwards sighs that move from low to high instead.

When you sing actual melodies you may experience more bumps at first. Slide as much as possible over the melodies at first to smooth out the bumps, then gradually work towards more pitch accuracy.

Warming Up

• Sing "Don't Know Why" on "yah," going for the yawn-sigh feeling you got with the sighing exercise. You can do one "yah" per word, stretch one "yah" over two notes or even over an entire phrase. Try all three ways to see which gives you the smoothest sound. At first stay very "slide-y," gliding down the melody in a relaxed way. Work with "yah" until you have smoothed out any register bumps. As always, your mouth will open more on the highest notes, then close up a bit on the lows. Make sure you don't close so much on the low notes that your "yah" sounds like "yuh." Some singers will find the high notes easy to attain in chest register, while many others will need to shift into head register.

• Sing the lyric, still sliding through the melody. Stay at a medium volume whether you are singing "yah" or the lyric, since that's the best volume for making a smooth transition from high to low and back again.

• Once you've smoothed out any register bumps you can work towards being more accurate with pitch. Try to find a balance of pitch accuracy and flowing sound. If register bumps appear, get slide-y again. Move back and forth from an overly slide-y to a "normal" version until all bumps have been erased.

• Another way you can help your voice through transition areas is to relax and exaggerate your enunciation at the same time. It's almost like you are chewing as you sing. This relaxes your tongue which in turn relaxes your throat, making it easier for your vocal cords to make adjustments. Just as above, if this works for you you'll then need to gradually work back to a less sloppy-sounding approach.

Troubleshooting

While the verse has a lot of relaxed descending melodies, on the bridge you need to sustain some high notes. Anticipating this is half the battle, so wake up and take a good breath right before the bridge, then support that first leap to "heart." Good diction will help, too. Here's the bridge lyric along with some diction notes:

My heart *(focus on "ah" and downplay the R)* is drenched in *(shape "ih")* wine *(shape "ah")*
But you'll *(focus on "oo" and downplay the L)* be on *(shape "ah")* my mind *(shape "ah" on both words)*
Forever *(loop the first R and downplay the second one, like faw-reh-vuhr)*

Expansion Ideas: Vibrato

Because it feels natural to sustain many of the phrase endings in "Don't Know Why," it's a good song to start exploring your use of vibrato. Done right, vibrato can add texture and shape to a line. Done wrong it can sound like a billy goat or an out of control wobble!

There are several ways to produce a vibrato, but to me the most natural sounding is the vibrato that slips in as you decrease the air pressure at the end of a line. Try singing a held note on the vowels "ee," "oo," and "ah" and gradually decrease the volume. Try not to let the sound get airy. This is a good way to encourage a vibrato to form if you don't have one. If you *do* have a vibrato, try to control the point at which you move from straight tone to vibrato. It may seem impossible at first but you can learn to release your throat and allow a vibrato to come in.

It's a common occurrence for beginning singers to have no vibrato at all, then after a week to a few months of voice work a vibrato just pops in. Give yourself time if you have no vibrato and want one; it will probably come as your vocal strength increases.

If you think you have too much of a vibrato, learning to control when it comes in with the above exercise can help. I'd also do a couple of low end songs (like "Summertime" and "Why Don't You Do Right?") daily where you sing with no vibrato at all. Sing them on "mee" for awhile to help control the vibrato, then try them with the lyrics. This will build more vocal strength.

Don't try to restrain your vibrato if you are concerned about relaxing your high notes. Letting a vibrato come out on high notes can help your throat relax. It's fine to sing with a fair amount of vibrato during the warming up part of your vocal work. Then when you are well warmed up you can work on controlling it.

Some singers find that their vibrato increases when they are in a mix register (the mix register is explained in the next chapter). This can work well in a jazz song like "Don't Know Why." A general rule of thumb for how much vibrato to use is to hold back on it until the final note of each phrase. But in songs with drawn out words like "Don't Know Why" it can sound good to use vibrato on some interior words, too, like the word "heart" early in the bridge. Check out Norah Jones' version and you'll hear a good example of mix register and vibrato.

Within almost every style of contemporary music you can find examples of singers who have almost no vibrato and singers with lots of it. How much vibrato to use is a personal choice.

Check out the version of "Don't Know Why" by Norah Jones

Don't Know Why

Jesse Harris

I waited 'til I saw the sun
I don't know why I didn't come
I left you by the house of fun
I don't know why I didn't come
I don't know why I didn't come

When I saw the break of day
I wished that I could fly away
Instead of kneeling in the sand
Catching teardrops in my hand

My heart is drenched in wine
But you'll be on my mind
Forever

Out across the endless sea
I would die in ecstasy
But I'll be a bag of bones
Driving down the road alone

My heart is drenched in wine
But you'll be on my mind
Forever

Something has to make you run
Don't know why I didn't come
I feel as empty as a drum
I don't know why I didn't come
I don't know why I didn't come
I don't know why I didn't come

Sunday Kind of Love

Focus: The Mix Register and More Register Navigation
Sound: Nyeah, Yeah
Alto/Bass Key: D
Baritone/Soprano Key: G

As I mentioned in the last chapter, there is a register in-between the chest and head register that is most commonly called the mix. Just to keep things straight here, I've also heard this register called the blend, the cover tone, and really confusingly, the head voice. The mix is a very useful register in that it allows you to move past your chest register with less of a change in sound quality than if you move to head voice. In most singers the mix sounds like a slightly thinner version of your chest voice. Norah Jones, Ella Fitzgerald, Barbra Streisand, Vince Gill, Natalie Cole, Mel Torme, Erikah Badu, and Steve Perry all use their mix register on their high notes, and rarely if ever use their head voice. Marvin Gaye and Eva Cassidy used all three registers, swooping from chest through mix to falsetto (head voice) and back again.

Please keep in mind that for most singers the mix is a register that needs to be coaxed into the voice—it took me three years with a teacher before I had any kind of handle on my mix register. On the other hand, I've seen very beginning singers attain a mix with a minimum of muss and fuss. If yours is a voice that seems to refuse to move into a mix register but goes directly into a head voice from chest voice, don't worry: let your voice do what it wants to do, use all the sounds that follow that will encourage your mix register to appear, and continue with the elastic, blended chest to head and back voice we worked on in the last song.

In real life you will hear mix register more in some styles than others. Jazz, soul, pop, show tunes, and R&B is where you'll hear it the most. It's less commonly heard in country and rock, but in those styles you'll often hear a half-mix/half-belt on high notes. I'll talk about that more in the final chapter. Belters and rock singers take heed: I strongly feel that warming up your highs in a mix register will best prepare you for the rigors of belting. Even if you never plan on using your mix register in your "real life" singing, your vocal cords will coordinate better if you learn how to sing in a mix. A perfect example of this is Sheryl Crow: I heard her sing a Burt Bacharach song a few years back with perfect mix notes on her highs. Singing her songs, however, she wants to sound more raw and less trained, so she pushes her chest voice as high as she can. I maintain that she gets away with this because she knows exactly what her voice is doing and that she could go into a mix at any point if she wanted to.

There is an upper limit to how high most singers can go in a mix. For most altos and sopranos it's around the F# an octave and a half above middle C, for most true basses it's an octave plus below that, around E above middle C. For most baritones and tenors it's around the B above middle C. Above these notes most singers need to move into head register. That means that once altos, baritones, and basses have found and strengthened their mix registers they may be able to stay in a mix when singing the highest notes in the workout. Sopranos, however, will probably need to switch into head register when singing the highest notes in the workout. This is the case with the high notes in the bridge of "Sunday Kind Of Love."

A small portion of the singers I've worked with attained a mix easily on open vowels like the "yah" you sang over "Don't Know Why." The majority of singers find it easier to first reach a mix on more nasal sounds. Unfortunately, the sound that seems to works best is one of the more awful sounds around, the very nasal sound "nyeah." Try to remember as you sing it that this is the means to an end. Once the mix is established you can work your way back to more open, less obnoxious sounds.

Make some loose "nyeah" sounds in the middle of your range, neither high nor low. It should sound like a cat or a nasty kid in the school yard, and it should resonate in the back of your nose and/or your soft palate (right behind the roof of your mouth). You're going for a very whiney sound here. If "nyeah" feels throaty or makes your jaw feel too tight, substitute "nay." Gradually work higher, noticing how the higher notes resonate behind your eyes. As you sing higher it should feel like the sound moves straight up the middle of your head, not forward.

Stay in a medium volume. On higher notes, if you sing loudly you'll tend to push your chest voice too high, and if you sing softly you might move into a head voice before you want to. Medium volume is the best volume for finding the mix register.

Working the Mix Register

• Sing each note of the melody on "nyeah." As you move from low to high notes you may feel the resonance move up from your soft palate to behind your nose and perhaps behind your eyes. Stay at a medium volume, and sing very quick, unsustained "nyeahs." As you get comfortable with the mix you can hold the notes longer. Sopranos will most likely move into head voice for the high notes of the bridge. The "nyeah" sound can also be used in head register to give the tone more clarity.

• When you feel like you are regularly singing in a mix on the higher notes you can try singing one of the less obnoxious sounds "yeah" or "nyah." Both of these are a bit nasal to help you retain the mix.

• Sing the lyric. The mix notes may seem a bit nasal at first, but will deepen with time.

Troubleshooting

If it seems harder to move through your registers when you sing the lyric, try sloppy or drunk singing for awhile.

You might sing a glottal attack on the high "I" that starts several of the phrases. Use a very light, almost invisible H to soften the attack. There's more on avoiding glottal attacks in the next chapter. Of course, think "ah" on those high "I"s.

Since the melody swoops frequently from high to low notes or the reverse, let your mouth open more on the highs, then close up a bit on the lows. This could happen fairly quickly from phrase to phrase.

There are a couple of tricky high words in the bridge. Slightly open towards an 'ih" on "scheming" to relax it, and downplay the R of "lover." Since "lover" falls on a high note that R will really stick out if you lean on it. The note on "lover" is the highest note in the workout so far. Stay at a medium volume, watch your breath support, and at first don't sustain the word.

Expansion Ideas

"Sunday Kind of Love" is a fun song on which to try "back-phrasing." That's when you start a phrase a bit later than usual. Billie Holiday was a master of back-phrasing, and Diana Krall is no slouch, either. I also hear back-phrasing frequently in rap music these days. As with your straight against swing phrasing on "I'm Beginning To See the Light," you'll be singing against the rhythmic groove. Back-phrasing can lend a very confident "I'll sing that note when I want to" feel to a song. Watch that you don't get so far behind the beat that your melody is falling on new chords that may clash. You can either start the melody late, then catch up by rushing the phrasing, or just keep the whole phrase behind the beat.

In case you're wondering, phrasing ahead of the beat can also be effective, especially on up-tempo songs. However, if you do it too much it can make your listener nervous. A combination of phrasing ahead and behind the beat on different phrases of a song might be a better bet.

Check out versions of "Sunday Kind of Love" by these singers:

Etta James • Dinah Washington • Natalie Cole • Louis Prima

Sunday Kind Of Love

Barbara Belle, Anita Leonard Nye, Louis Prima & Stanley Rhodes

I want a Sunday kind of love
A love to last past Saturday night
I'd like to know it's more than love at first sight
I want a Sunday kind of love

I want a love that's on the square
Can't seem to find somebody to care
I'm on a lonely road that leads me nowhere
I want a Sunday kind of love

I do my Sunday dreaming
And all my Sunday scheming
Every minute, every hour, every day
I'm hopin' to discover
A certain kind of lover
Who will show me the way

My arms need someone to enfold
To keep me warm when Mondays are cold
A love for all my life
To have and to hold
I want a Sunday kind of love

Thank You

Focus: The Inner Smile
Sound: Nah
Alto/Bass Key: B
Baritone/Soprano Key: F

I bet you're sick of that "nyeah" sound, right? Now you can move away from the overly nasal sounds towards something that's a little more balanced. "Nah" is a sound that combines the helpful nasality of "nyeah" with the openness of "ah."

Another element that will help you find the right balance of nasality and openness is the "inner smile." I mentioned your soft palate a few chapters ago; that's the spot right behind your hard palate that lifts up when you yawn. Go ahead and yawn since I'm talking about it, and as you do see if you feel a lifting sensation. Some singers also feel the soft palate lift when they inhale through their nose. It feels like a muscle that can't be controlled, but actually it can. Keep noticing how it feels the next time you yawn, then immediately do a yawn-sigh and see if you can lift the soft palate up slightly at will. Try an ascending yawn-sigh as well. Slightly lifting the soft palate can open your throat and sinuses, making it easier to hit high notes. It can also add a nice "ring" to your tone. Don't go too far with lifting your soft palate or you'll sound like on Barney on "The Simpsons"! Ideally, your soft palate will slightly lift as you inhale, then remain lifted as you vocalize.

Watch yourself in the the mirror as you inhale through your nose and lift your eyebrows. It may feel like the upper half of your face is opening and lifting as you inhale, and you may also feel your soft palate lift. This is the "inner smile." You should look like someone is telling you the most interesting story you ever heard. On the exhale as you yawn-sigh "nah" keep everything lifted. This will keep resonance on your low notes and smooth your transition downward. Try this again, this time breathing in through your mouth. Feel the air pass across your soft palate as you inhale, then feel the resonance in your soft palate and behind your nose and eyes as you sigh out "nah".

Inhale one more time and sing "nah" again, with one addition. As before, feel the sound move up through your soft palate to the back of your eyes, but now imagine that the sound is arcing out through your eyes. This gives you a balanced tone that projects out.

Warming Up

• Sing the melody on "nah," trying to notice the inner smile as you sing. You probably won't notice the yawn-sigh feeling until the beginning of the chorus, but throughout the song you should feel a gentle lifting in the upper half of your face. It's fine to slide one "nah" over two notes if you want. Another benefit of the inner smile is that it helps keep low notes facially placed. It's okay if you close up so much on the lows that you're singing "nuh" instead of "nah."

• Sing the lyric. The "I" that rises at the beginning of the chorus can be in chest voice, mix, or head voice. Regardless of the vocal register, using the inner smile can make high notes easier. When you are first working the song, slide between the two notes on "I." Later you can shoot for more pitch accuracy.

Troubleshooting

There are three diphthongs on the chorus that fall on higher notes. On "I" shape "ah" with your mouth, on "oh" shape "aw", and on "day" shape "eh."

Watch out for glottal attacks, which are a slight grabbing of the vocal cords that tend to happen when a high word starts with a vowel, like the "I" and "oh" in the chorus. Glottal attacks can add an unpleasant percussiveness to your singing, and they will tire your voice out very quickly. If you do them for a desired effect, do them on purpose, not by accident. A lot of glottal attacks in one's singing can also be a sign of vocal fatigue. Sometimes looping can erase a glottal attack, but that isn't an option when a phrase starts with a vowel. In that case, add an invisible H to the "I", just enough to cushion the attack, not so much that it becomes "Hi." Using the inner smile to add a bit more nasal resonance to your sound can also help. Shaking your head "no" as you sing can relax your throat and lessen the chance of a glottal attack, but don't do that when you're performing unless you are Stevie Wonder.

If the song seems to be moving by too quickly to manage the notes, hit your pause button and try singing it a cappella at a steady but slower tempo.

Sometimes it's not the notes but the rhythm that makes a song difficult to learn. Syncopated lines like the first line of "Thank You" have many notes that fall on the off-beat. Here's the first line with all of the off-beats underlined. If you tap your feet or play a metronome while you sing or recite the lyrics in rhythm you'll hear how they fall in-between the beats:

My tea's gone cold, I'm won-d'ring why I got out of bed at all

Tapping while you sing can help you feel and learn the syncopated lines faster.

If you know Dido's version of "Thank You" you may remember that she lets her voice break on the word "I" at the top of the chorus. That's a good example of using a register break for an artistic effect instead of hiding it. It also helps her delineate each note of "I" so that she doesn't slide in-between them. (I know I told you to slide on those notes, but that's for warm up purposes only.) If you want to copy her break, try singing louder on the chest voice lower note of "I," then pull back on the volume as you leap to the higher note. You can also imagine that the note is suddenly shifting from resonating in your mouth to your eyes. A third trick is to tilt your head down as you shift into head voice. Singing tilted over can work well for adding body to a breathy head voice. You'll lose a bit of resonance when you stand up straight again but your tone and placement should feel better. Maintain the inner smile for all these methods.

If the higher note doesn't comfortably fall into your head voice you can create the same effect by deliberately singing softer and breathier on the higher note. You can also do this if both notes fall in your head voice or mix.

Another way to speed the leap on the "I" so that it isn't too slide-y is to use this singer's trick: pull your abdomen in suddenly as you go for the higher note. This could backfire and cause you to overshoot the note, but it's worth trying.

Expansion Ideas

If you're familiar with Dido's version of "Thank You" you might have noticed an airy or velvety quality to her tone, which I went for on my version (Perry the baritone does a cleaner tone on his version but baritones and sopranos can listen to the style section on CD #2 to hear an example of an airier tone). Norah Jones and Sting are two other singers who sometimes mix a lot of air into their tone. The best way to get that sound is to waste some air while you sing, releasing some extra air along with the tone. This is also a good way to add some texture, or even grit, to your voice. Make sure you have lots of facial resonance to combine with the air, so the tone has some substance. The extra air might dry out your throat a bit but it's much easier on your voice and body than other methods like smoking a pack of cigarettes! Keep in mind that since you're wasting some air you won't have as much sustenance. I prefer to warm up with a cleaner tone, then add some airiness if it's appropriate when I'm stylizing the song.

Thank You

Paul Herman & Dido

My tea's gone cold, I'm wondering why I got out of bed at all
The morning rain clouds up my window and I can't see at all
And even if I could it'd all be grey, but your picture on my wall
It reminds me that it's not so bad
It's not so bad

I drank too much last night, got bills to pay
My head just feels in pain
I missed the bus and there'll be hell today
I'm late for work again
And even if I'm there, they'll all imply
That I might not last the day
And then you call me and it's not so bad
And it's not so bad

I want to thank you
For giving me the best day of my life
Oh just to be with you
Is having the best day of my life

Push the door, I'm home at last
And I'm soaking through and through
Then you handed me a towel and all I see is you
And even if my house falls down now, I wouldn't have a clue
Because you're near me and—

I want to thank you
For giving me the best day of my life
Oh just to be with you
Is having the best day of my life

You're Still the One

Focus: Stepwise and Larger Interval Pitch Work
Sound: Dee, Dah
Alto/Bass Key: Eb
Baritone/Soprano Key: A

Early on in the workout I recommended that you not focus on pitch accuracy unless your sense of pitch was really shaky. Now that your voice is well warmed up it's time to do some pitch work. A while back I was talking to a professional singer friend of mine who seemed to have flawless intonation (which means having good pitch or singing in tune). I asked her if she was one of those rare singers who had always sung in tune, and she answered that the singers she knew who had great intonation were the ones who worked on it regularly.

With the advent of pitch correction studio technology we continually hear flawless intonation pouring from our radios and CD players. Not only can a singer's pitch be "fixed in the mix" when they record a vocal, but on-board pitch correction can be used to fix sour notes at live shows. You just don't know who can sing in tune anymore unless you hear them sing unamplified or you know that pitch correction wasn't used. I've started to welcome hearing a few off notes at live shows since it tells me that pitch correction isn't being used!

If you listen to recordings from the 60s and earlier you'll hear some really off notes coming from great singers like Frank Sinatra and Billie Holiday, and every year at the Grammies I hear famous singers hit real clunkers. It's not the end of the world if you hit a bad note, almost everyone does. We all want to sing in tune and it's important to work pitch, but don't let it drive you crazy.

Let me distinguish between two kinds of pitch problems. The most common intonation problems are technical: you can hear the note just fine, but when you sing it the note comes out wrong, usually flat or slightly under the right note. This is an ear/brain/vocal cord coordination issue that can be fixed with good voice technique and practice. Dozens of singers have come to me thinking that they were tone deaf when they just needed a little bit of voice technique.

Very occasionally a singer really can't hear notes well. Though I've coached well over a thousand singers, I've encountered only two that may actually have been tone-deaf. Both of them had zero exposure to music as children so even with them I don't know if the problem was nature or nurture. When a singer can't hear notes well they can still improve, but progress comes more slowly. Working with a voice teacher may be necessary, and piano lessons can also help to strengthen one's ear.

A few years ago I tested my brother during a visit. I sang some notes and he couldn't sing them back or even tell me which ones were higher or lower. I told him to find an easy listening radio station and to only sing along with slow easy songs sung by male singers so the songs were in his range. I had him hum the songs first, then sing them on "dee", then the words. He came back a year later singing complete melodies in tune. His tone wasn't bad, either!

Since the vast majority of singers are not tone-deaf and just need to do a bit of intonation work, I'm going to focus on that. Keep in mind that many elements outside of how much you've been practicing can effect your sense of pitch. Your body is your instrument, so body changes can temporarily mess with your ability to sing in tune. Allergies, lack of sleep, menstruation, and depression can all cause you to go off-key, usually flat. Bad sound systems or "dead," unresonant rooms can make it difficult to hear. You know how it's easier to hear yourself sing in the shower or the car? That's because you're in a small space and your sound is bouncing off the tile or windshield right back at you.

Bad voice technique also contributes to pitch problems. Sudden volume surges or too much effort can cause you to sing sharp, or above the note. Throat tension and lack of breath support are common reasons singers will hit a flat note. Overly relaxed, unfocussed notes can also slip, and control and placement help this. Interestingly, I've worked with a few singers who had too much of a nasal sound. Their tone wasn't good but their pitch was great, I think because the added nasal resonance was easier for them to hear. In contrast, singers with very open, airy tones (like Sade, for example) can have more difficulty hearing. Adding just a bit of nasal resonance to those tones can make it easier to sing in tune.

Another common accuracy problem is "scooping." Most often if a singer hits an off note it is flat, not sharp. As soon as the singer hears the note they scoop up to correct it. Scooping is very common and works in a lot of styles like blues, country, and jazz. The danger is in developing a habit of always scooping when you sing. Eventually you'll sing a song where scooping isn't appropriate and you'll be in trouble. I'd recommend singing at least a couple of songs a day with very little if any scooping, just to keep your chops up. That's what "You're Still the One" and "Ms. Celie's Blues" are for.

I'm very good at hearing pitch problems in other singers but not as good at hearing them in myself. When I'm working pitch on a song I tape myself and listen back. If you do this, work with the lyric sheet and underline the words that sound off-key. You may notice that words containing certain vowels are the hardest ones for you. These problem vowels fluctuate from singer to singer, but some I've noticed are "uh," "ih," and "oh." If you find a vowel that is hard for you to tune, put a D in front of it (like "duh," "dih," and "doh,") and sing entire songs with that sound.

Working Pitch with "You're Still the One"

• Sing on "dee" or "dah". Most singers find that "dee" is the easiest to use when working pitch accuracy, so start with that if possible. Substitute “dih” on the high notes if you need to. Use one "dee" or "dah" per note. If a word or syllable is stretched out over three notes give each of the notes a "dee" or "dah."

1) No more sliding between notes. Go for a very accurate, almost robot-like version.

2) If you are using CD #1, listen to the vocal and try to lock in with each note. If that's easy to do then focus on the accompaniment as you sing, noticing how the melody and accompaniment work together. Do this also if you're working with CD #2.

3) Though you should focus on the accompaniment when you're singing, you do need to be able to hear yourself. If you can't, cup one or both hands behind (not over) your ears. Or, if possible, move to a more reverberant room like your kitchen or bathroom. Working on headphones is useful, too.

• Sing the lyric. Start off with very accurate pitch and a robot delivery, then gradually relax into a more normal, flowing version. Advanced singers can skip the robot part.

Troubleshooting

• If you are going flat:

Try nose inhalations and the inner smile, check your breath support, and make sure that your throat is relaxed.

• If you are going sharp:

Relax your throat on each inhalation (gently touch your larynx and try to feel it dropping), pull back on your volume, and work with more open sounds like "dah" or "duh."

The verse has some big leaps that you should watch out for. Surprisingly, it's the leaps to lower notes that can be hard. Since the vocal cords relax as you descend to lower notes it's easy to over-relax and overshoot the note. I equate it with driving backwards down a hill: backing down a hill by releasing the brakes is much harder to control than using the accelerator to climb the hill. If you are singing the lyric, closing your mouth up a bit on the lower words will help you control them. Make sure those low notes are placed—if they aren't, hum them or substitute higher notes.

The chorus is filled with descending stepwise melodies. Stepwise melodies are easier to sing than big leaps, but watch these anyway since they are descending. Some singers tend to go flat on the "I" of "You're still the one I..." which occurs three times per chorus, so watch out for those notes. The song doesn't go as high as some of your previous songs so even though there are some melodic leaps up they shouldn't be too hard to manage with practice.

Watch out for the three note melisma on the word "to" halfway through the chorus. A melisma is when a syllable or word is carried over three or more notes. Accuracy is easier when there is one word per note, which is the case for most of the song. It's easy to slide over and lose accuracy on melismas. Make sure the middle of the three notes doesn't go flat.

Expansion Ideas

Since you're focussing on intonation with "You're Still the One," back off on stylizing. Some singers use a bluesy style to disguise their intonation problems. If you just have to add some fills, use this one to practice passing tones, neighboring tones and appoggiaturas, and make sure they are as accurate as the rest of the song.

Check out the version of "You're Still the One" by Shania Twain (who, by the way, uses on-board pitch correction whenever she performs!)

You're Still the One

Shania Twain & R.J. Lange

Looks like we made it
Look how far we've come my baby
We mighta took the long way
We knew we'd get there someday
They said, "I bet they'll never make it"
But just look at us holding on
We're still together still going strong

You're still the one I run to
The one that I belong to
You're still the one I want for life
You're still the one that I love
The only one I dream of
You're still the one I kiss good night

Ain't nothin' better
We beat the odds together
I'm glad we didn't listen
Look at what we would be missin'
They said, "I bet they'll never make it"
But just look at us holding on
We're still together still going strong

You're still the one I run to
The one that I belong to
You're still the one I want for life
You're still the one that I love
The only one I dream of
You're still the one I kiss good night

Looks like we made it
Look how far we've come my baby

Tracks of My Tears

Focus: Sustenance, Volume, Singing High Closed Vowels
Sounds: Lee, Yeah, Wo
Alto/Bass Key: Ab
Baritone/Soprano Key: Db

Now that your voice is warmed up and you've worked intonation a bit, you can work on strengthening other vocal areas like sustenance, volume, and singing high closed vowels. If you've been maintaining good singer's posture and correct breathing all the way through the workout, then you've been working on sustenance the whole time. Now you can test your limits on a song with long phrases.

If your breathing has slipped a bit while concentrating on other vocal matters, now is a good time to get your support happening again. Relax on your inhalation, keep your rib cage up on the exhalation, this time counting in a sloppy singsong until you are out of air. Stop counting as soon as you sense any throat tension or better yet, slightly before. You can do this to pass the time when you're stuck in traffic. Try to increase how long you count each day.

Good facial resonance will also help you sustain notes longer since it gives you more sound with less effort. It also helps you use air more efficiently. An overly breathy voice (like Marilyn Monroe's) wastes a lot of air.

Good diction can also increase sustenance. Try singing some long held notes on different vowel sounds, making little adjustments in your jaw position and mouth shape. You may find a resonant, comfortable "sweet spot" for each vowel where it feels like you could hold the note for a minute.

The thing that will mess with your sustenance the most is worrying too much about it. If you think you will run out of air early you probably will. So if you have to breathe, breathe. I find myself holding notes the longest when I'm performing and not thinking about it. Unfortunately, while you are building vocal strength you may need to be fairly self-conscious about what you're doing. This may sometimes translate into subtle tension that shortens your sustain. This is an interim situation. Your ultimate goal is to train your body through continued practice so that it remembers how to sing correctly. Then when you sing you can stay focused on the lyric and the instrument to which you are tuning. That's when you'll sing long phrases effortlessly.

Warming Up

• Sing "Tracks of My Tears" on the sounds "lee," "yeah," or "wo". On high notes use the more open sounds "yeah" or "wo." You may find that your air lasts longest on "lee" and shortest on "wo." If one sound seems to be easier to sustain than another, stick with it.

• Sing the lyric. If possible, sing the entire first phrase ("People say I'm the life of the party 'cause I tell a joke or two") on one breath. Do the same on the second phrase. If you run out of air and are squeezing the last few words out, catch a breath somewhere during the phrase until your sustenance increases.

Troubleshooting

On the chorus there are several melodic leaps to high notes. The first one is on the word "good." Open almost to an "eh" shape and pucker your lips, keeping them soft. On "smile," the second high note, shape "ah," and loop the "l" in "smile" over to the "l" of "looks." When you have back-to-back consonants like that you only need to pronounce one of them. Shape "aw" on "closer," the high note of the third phrase, and do the same on the extended rising "oh" that follows that phrase. The next phrase has high notes on the words "need you." Both have closed vowels, and singing closed vowels on high notes gets a section of its own:

Singing High Closed Vowels

It's much harder for most people to sing a high mixed or chest voice "ee" or "oo" than any other vowel, because "ee" and "oo" are closed vowels. You already know to drop your jaw more on these vowels when they fall on high notes. Here's another way to open them, using the inner smile:

- Inhale through your nose and feel your soft palate lift
- Sing "mah" on a high sustained note
- Close the front of your mouth until the vowel changes from "ah" to "ee" while keeping the lift in your soft palate. You will still have a slight gap between your upper and lower teeth.

If you've been squeezing your high "ees" on the word "need" in the last line of the chorus, this should feel much better. To work high "oos," like the word "you" at the end of the bridge, do the above exercise and add this additional step:

- As you maintain the same gap between your teeth and keep your soft palate lifted, let your lips come forward to shape "oo." Don't let your tongue retract as your lips move forward.

The last phrase of the bridge requires some sustenance and ends on a high note. Get a catch breath if you need one, it's better to do that than run out of air on the word "you."

For those of you familiar with the original version, I've combined some of the back-up vocals in the bridge with the lead melody.

Building Volume

I've recommended that you stay at a medium volume on the first eleven workout songs. Now is a good time to work at a louder volume. Increased vocal volume comes primarily from three sources: good breath support, strong vocal cords, and facial resonance. You've been working on all three as you sing through the workout. If you usually speak softly or have always sung in a soft to medium volume, your vocal cords may not have the strength for suddenly very loud notes. When you're doing volume work, increase very gradually from a medium volume, continually monitoring your throat for tension.

Try singing some loose sounds before you tackle "Tracks of My Tears" with more volume. First, stand up and do some quick abdominal pushes to activate your support muscles. To do this, put your hand on your belly and pull in sharply with your abdominal muscles, causing the air to rush out of your mouth. I call these pushes because you are pushing the air out with your adominals. If you engage your vocals cords it should sound like a light laugh. Make sure your throat stays relaxed and that your abdominals are doing the pushing.

Find an object at least ten feet away on which you can focus. Now push from your abdominals and exclaim the word "yeah!" in the middle of your range, at a medium volume. Imagine the arcing of resonance you worked on earlier: the sound moves up through the middle of your head and out your eyes, towards your focal point. Again, check your throat for tension. Continue to call out "yeah!," gradually increasing your volume each time. Back off if your throat gets overly involved. Try the same calling with the words "hey!" and "wo!"

The sudden belly push is not something you should do when you're normally singing, since you want your support muscles to give you constant steady support. It's more of a device to make sure that you're supporting the sound as you go for increased volume. However, it is a trick that some singers use if they are going for a high note.

Another concept that will prevent your throat from tightening as you add volume is to imagine that your larynx is tipping forward as you project. This can help keep the larynx from rising in your throat when you increase your volume.

Adding Volume to "Tracks of My Tears"

The higher you sing, the louder your voice will naturally grow. You should never try to force more volume on very low notes, you'll just strain. The chorus of "Tracks of My Tears" sits higher than the rest of the song, so increase your volume there. Go back to medium volume on verse 2 to give yourself a rest before the next chorus. Try the song with the warm-up sounds first since they are easier. If singing them with more volume feels fine, switch to the lyric. You can use some of the tricks you used earlier in the workout to keep your throat relaxed as you add volume, like singing sloppy or slowly shaking "no" as you sing. The latter won't work well if you're also trying to arc the sound out towards a focal point, however.

Expansion Ideas

The verses of "Tracks of My Tears" are fairly wordy and don't have a lot of room for ornamentation. One way to stylize melodies like these is to substitute an alternate note during the melody. For example, on the first line "People say I'm the life of the party," try singing "life" on the same note as "say." Try to do substitutions on more important words like "life" rather than little words like "the" or "a." I'd only do one or two substitutions per phrase so you retain most of the original melody unless you are really jazzing up a song.

Check out "Tracks of My Tears" by these singers:

Smokey Robinson • Linda Ronstadt

Tracks of My Tears

Warren Moore, Smokey Robinson & Marvin Tarplin

People say I'm the life of the party
'Cause I tell a joke or two
Although I might be laughin' loud and hearty
Deep inside I'm blue

So take a good look at my face
You'll see my smile looks out of place
If you look closer it's easy to trace
The tracks of my tears
Whoah--I need you, need you

Since you left me if you see me with another girl
Seemin' like I'm havin' fun
Although she may be cute
She's just a substitute
'Cause you're the permanent one

So take a good look at my face
You'll see my smile looks out of place
If you look closer it's easy to trace
The tracks of my tears
Whoah--

Outside, I'm masquerading
Inside, my hope is fading
Just a clown, yeah
Since you put me down
My smile is my makeup
I wear since my breakup with you

Baby, take a good look at my face
You'll see my smile looks out of place
If you look closer it's easy to trace
The tracks of my tears

Ms. Celie's Blues (Sister)

Focus: Chromatic Pitch Work
Sound: Dee, Dah
Alto/Bass Key: C
Baritone/Soprano Key: F

Many melodies are scale-based and move in what is called stepwise motion up or down the scale. The line "Life is but a dream" from "Row, Row, Row Your Boat" moves in stepwise motion down a major scale. Most singers find stepwise based melodies easier to sing than melodies that have huge leaps in them or chromatic melodies. Chromatic melodies have two elements that make them harder to sing. Chromatic lines move in half-steps, which is the smallest interval between two adjacent notes. The vocal cords must make a very small adjustment to navigate a half-step and so they are easy to overshoot. Chromatic melodies also step outside the key of the song, making it harder to lock into the music.

Here's some brief music theory that should explain why some notes are harder to tune than others. Keep in mind that if you are singing with CD #1 you have a melody line to follow. On CD #2 and in real life the training wheels are off and you are singing the melody while the band (or guitar or piano) accompanies you with chords.

I'll use Eb, the alto/bass key of "You're Still the One," for this example, but the following would hold for any key. In the key of Eb you have seven notes, Eb, F, G, Ab, Bb, C, and D. Those notes comprise the scale of Eb. Eb, G and Bb are the notes in the chord of Eb. If a melody note you are singing is also in the chord being played you can feel that they match, or lock together. For example, the note on "it" in "Looks like we made it" in the first line of "You're Still the One" is also in the chord being played. It feels resolved, like you are home. If your melody note is from the scale of Eb but not in the chord being played, like the first word "made" in "Looks like we made it," you'll hear a slight but not unpleasant dissonance between the note and the chord. Since the entire melody of "You're Still the One" stays in the key of Eb it all sounds like it works, though the melody notes that are not in the chord being played might be a little harder to lock due to the slight dissonance.

You don't have to lock every note you sing to the chord being sung, of course. I'm just pointing out why some notes are harder to lock to a chord than others. You also stay in tune by remembering the exact distances or intervals between notes: that's how a cappella singers keep from straying. When you have an accompanist, however, I think it's important to focus on them. Listening to yourself as you sing can send you off-key. As you sing, feel what you're body is doing as you listen to the accompaniment. Another idea: one of my teachers, Judy Davis, told me that 5% of a singer's attention should be on the accompaniment to stay in tune, while the remaining 95% of one's focus should be on what the lyric is saying.

Chromatic lines move in half-steps and one or more of the notes step outside the key of the song. If you sustained that note against the chord being played you would hear a very dissonant sound that really rubs, not the slight dissonance of a scale note against a chord. "My" in the first line of "Sister", "Sister, you've been on my mind," is one of these notes. Really dissonant notes like these that step outside of the song's key can be harder to tune since they rub against the chord so much. It's probably better to practice and memorize the sound of chromatic lines. "Ms. Celie's Blues" has a lot of chromatic movement and is a good song for that. Even if you only sing scale-based rock songs that have no chromatic movement in them, singing chromatic lines is a great musicianship exercise. My college music theory professor David Cope called this "practicing with a lead softball": you sing something that is very difficult to tune, then when you sing an easier scale-based song it's a piece of cake.

Working Pitch with "Ms. Celie's Blues"

• Sing with "dee," then "dah." Drop your jaw towards "dih" if the high "dees" are uncomfortable. As you did with "You're Still the One" go for very accurate intonation. Use one "dee" or "dah" per note.

• This is optional: try long extended "dee's" or "dah's" that cover several notes. Doing this accurately is much harder, so it's a great intonation exercise.

• Sing the lyric. There are almost no melismas in "Ms. Celie's Blues," so it's possible that this will be easier to do than singing an extended "dah" over the melody.

Troubleshooting

Here's an idea for working harder melodies. Use your hand to physicalize the vocal movement. When notes rise lift your hand, when they fall lower your hand. Sometimes externalizing the melody like this helps your vocal accuracy. It's a common method used by many gospel singers and pop/r&b singers like Mariah Carey.

Keep those chromatic lines accurate. Hit the pause button on your CD player if necessary and work them a cappella if you need to.The chromatic lines are underlined on the lyric.

All of the words in bold are notes that fall outside of the chords of "Ms. Celie's Blues." That means they will feel more dissonant and may be harder to tune.

Open the "ih" of "sister" as much as you can (without turning it into "sehster") when it falls on high notes, like the first note of the song.

"Suns goin' down" on the bridge hits some very low notes. If going a bit nasal and closing up on the words still doesn't place them, stay on the note you sing on "lot" for the rest of "lot of suns goin' down."

Expansion Ideas

Stylistically, "Ms. Celie's Blues" is a bluesy jazz song. Both blues and jazz have a lot of scooping and sliding in them. It's fine to slide around the notes more if you are working on a performance version of "Ms. Celie's Blues," but if you are doing it for intonation practice stay more accurate. Instead, try some phrasing ideas where you sing fragments of phrases either faster or slower. In the first line try slowing down "on my mind," then come in late and rush the phrase on "two of a kind."

Check out Shug's (Tata Vega's) version of "Ms. Celie's Blues" in the movie "The Color Purple" to hear back-phrasing, and a good mix register on the high notes.

Miss Celie's Blues (Sister)

Quincy Jones, Lionel Richie & Rodney Temperton

Sister, you've **been** on **my** mind
Sister, we're two of a **kind**
So sister
I'm keepin' **my** eye **on** you
I **bet**cha **think** I **don't** know nothin'
But **sing**in' **the** blues
Oh sister, have I got **news for** you
I'm somethin'
I hope you **think** that you´re some**thin'** too

Scufflin',
I been up that lonesome **road**
And I seen a lot of suns **go**in' down
Oh, but trust me
No low life's gonna **run** me **a**round

So **let** me **tell** you **some**thin' sister
Remember **your** name
No twister gonna **steal** your stuff away
My sister
We sure ain't **got** a whole **lot** of time
So shake **your** shimmy
Sister
'Cause honey the **shug** is **feel**in' fine

Alison

Focus: Adding Richness, Consonant Articulation
Sound: Duh, Nuh
Alto/Bass Key: C
Baritone/Soprano Key: E

The trickiest thing about singing well might be the balancing act of relaxation and control that your body must constantly maintain. Too relaxed and your pitch could go flat or your enunciation could be sloppy. Too controlled and you could tense up your throat and face, causing voice strain or a tight sound. When you're singing well you'll find that parts of your body, like your belly and throat as you inhale, will feel relaxed. At the same time other parts of your body, like your lifted rib cage, will feel firm.

With "Alison" you're going to follow this theme as we return to the area of throat relaxation and resonance, and you'll also focus on consonant articulation.

It's very possible that as you sang through the workout song by song that you easily assimilated each new area of study. But some of us can get caught up in an area like volume or pitch work and not notice that we've tensed up our throats in the process. If that's the situation for you, singing a ballad like "Alison" at a medium volume can help you regain any tonal richness you might have lost. Remember, if your throat tightens you might be restricting the sound waves that your vocal cords produce. If your tongue or face tenses up the sound may not resonate fully.

"Duh" is a sound that causes your tongue to round and relax, which in turn helps your throat to let go. Singing "duh" tends to produce a richer tone than most other sounds. Sung at a medium volume, "duh" can fatten your tone and re-relax your sound if it needs it. The slightly more nasal "nuh" can substitute for "duh" if you want to try a different sound. Use whichever sound works best for you.

Warming Up

- Sing "Alison" with "duh" or "nuh" at a medium volume until the melody is both relaxed and accurate. Use the inner smile with "duh" so that your throat, jaw, and tongue are relaxed, while your soft palate and upper half of your face feel open and lifted.

- Sing the lyric.

Troubleshooting

The chorus is the hard part of "Alison," right from the high first note on the A of "Alison." Use an invisible H to avoid a glottal attack. Use the natural nasality of the vowel to get good facial placement, but also drop your jaw enough and use your inner smile on the A to keep it from being too nasal.

The "you" at the end of the phrase "I know this world is killing you" can be difficult because it ends high. Drop your jaw a bit and make sure your upper lip is puckered and soft. That phrase usually continues right into "Oh, Alison" without a breath, but catch one before "oh" or "Alison" if you need to.

Feel free to slow down or even eliminate the fast three note melismas that occur at the ends of several phrases in the verse and chorus (like the end of "Oh, Alison") if they are too fast to do accurately.

Articulation

If you haven't done it already, now is a good time to pay attention to articulation, or the enunciation of consonants. How much or how little to articulate a consonant is a matter of taste and style, ranging from the very precise articulation of musical theater to the very relaxed articulation of blues. The median point between these will work for many styles, including pop, country, rock, and jazz. For these you want light, crisp but natural sounding consonants, neither over nor under-pronounced. This is tricky, because as soon as you detect that one consonant or another is lazy you'll tend to overdo it for awhile. Sometimes speaking the word in question helps you feel the right amount to articulate.

There are several consonants or consonant combinations that are easy to get sloppy on, like V, N, ND, and NG. Which consonants might be more difficult is an individual thing that has to do with the size of your tongue, shape of your teeth, etc. The best thing to do is to record yourself and analyze which consonants might be troublesome. You can even sing songs with words containing your trouble consonants: my weakest consonants are M and B, so sometimes I sing a little ditty called "Bombing Mom and bombing Malibu"!

For crisp articulation you may have to use your tongue, teeth and lips more than you're used to. As always, practice helps. The balancing act here is to use your mouth enough for good articulation while keeping your throat relaxed for maximum resonance.

An aside about some aggressive styles of music: I've worked with musical theater, heavy metal and punk rock singers who wanted to express anger in their songs. The problem was that they always constricted their throats when they did. Here's what I think works best whenever a singer is conveying a strong emotion: try to feel that the emotion is coming from your gut, same as your support muscles. Then shoot the sound up through your open throat to the front of your mouth, where you can over-articulate to increase the intensity of the emotion. Elvis Costello, the writer and original performer of "Alison," demonstrates this technique very well in many of his songs. On angry songs he practically spits the words out. He delivers intensity without suffering vocal fatigue: I saw him do a two hour live show last year and his voice was stronger than ever after a twenty-five year career.

Expansion Ideas

I'm sure you've heard singers that are all style but no substance. After they sing you remember that they did some great vocal acrobatics but you wonder why you weren't moved. The whole point of stylizing a song is to bring out the lyric and to make your delivery sound authentic, not forced. There are some ways to aim for this as you stylize a song. First of all, less is more. Over-ornamenting can ruin a song. It's fine to go to town when you are in the experimental stage of song stylizing, but eventually you should record yourself and listen to see if your fills are really enhancing the song. Also, try to avoid repeating the same ornament over and over. That will just call attention to the ornament and not the song.

Which words you choose to ornament or phrase can make your delivery sound more natural. In general, use words that you would emphasize when speaking. When in doubt, speak the phrase to find out which word or syllable has the inflection, then if possible ornament that word. Adjectives and action verbs are often good bets, as are expressive words like "oh" or "baby."

Your inflection on ornaments is also important. Try to emphasize the first note of the ornament more than the rest. You can even let your voice fade or go breathy after the first note to make the ornament sound more off the cuff. Fast ornaments can also sound nicely tossed off. If you slow them down too much it can be like you're saying "look what I can do!" When you're learning different ornaments, however, sing them slowly to make sure they are accurate.

Try speaking the lines of "Alison" to find out which words might best be ornamented. There are no set rules for this since a sentence can be spoken many ways. Then try some passing tones, appoggiaturas, neighboring tones and substitution notes on these words. You might have to phrase the line differently to make room for the ornament. For instance, in the chorus try an ornament on the words "know," "killing," and "oh." Whether your interpretation works subjective, so you'll be the ultimate judge.

Alison

Elvis Costello

Oh, it's so funny to be seeing you after so long, girl
And with the way you look I understand that you are not impressed
But I heard you let that little friend of mine take off your party dress
I'm not gonna to get too sentimental
Like those other sticky valentines
'Cause I don't know if you are loving somebody
I only know it isn't mine

Alison
I know this world is killing you
Oh, Alison
My aim is true

Well I see you've got a husband now
Did he leave your pretty fingers lying in the wedding cake?
You used to hold him right in your hand
I bet he took all he could take
Sometimes I wish that I could stop you from talking
When I hear the silly things that you say
I think somebody better put out the big light
'Cause I can't stand to see you this way

Alison
I know this world is killing you
Oh, Alison
My aim is true

I Hope You Dance

Focus: Ending On High Notes
Sound: Yeah, Yah
Alto/Bass Key: Bb
Baritone/Soprano Key: F

"I Hope You Dance"" has another vocal challenge for you: the first line of the chorus ends on a sustained high note. Most singers find that sustaining and ending high notes is difficult, since your vocal cords have shortened to vibrate faster on higher notes. It requires more vocal strength and awareness so that your throat doesn't become overly involved. You have a few choices here. You can simply end the note at the same volume with which you attacked it, fade the note to a softer volume, or add vibrato to finish the note. If it takes a lot of strength for you to reach the high note you may not be able to fade or add vibrato, since both of these require some dexterity and strength that not all singers have. Some singers who can't fade a high note just fade their sound by gradually pulling away from the microphone. Others will add a fill like a descending passing tone to the melody which gets them to a lower, easier note on which to end. This is what happens in the actual chorus melody on "I Hope You Dance," but if you want, you can skip the passing tone and end on the high note. Perry White and I do that at least once each on our workout versions.

Working High Notes with "I Hope You Dance"

• Sing the song with either "yeah" or "yah," whichever one you like the most. "Yah" is more open and might be easier on the high notes, but "yeah" has a nasality that can encourage good placement, plus it has the vowel sound you'll be sustaining on the word "dance" when you switch to the lyric. You don't have to put a Y on every note, you can occasionally stretch one "yeah" or "yah" over two notes if you prefer. See the paragraph on ending high on the word "dance" if you have any problems.

• Sing the lyric.

Troubleshooting

The "I" that starts the song is on a high note. Support it, shape "ah" and use an invisible H so you don't grab it. Some of the other high notes in the verse are on closed vowels, so keep your soft palate slightly lifted and drop your jaw a bit to relax them.

Downplay the Rs that fall on high notes like "never" and "fear" in the verse. Downplay the Ls that do the same, like in "still feel small." Loop the words to keep them flowing.

Ending High on the Word "Dance"

Volume often naturally increases as you ascend, but if you swell too much you could push your chest voice too high and end up yelling the high note. Try to stay at a medium or medium loud volume. Make sure that your attack on the word "dance" feels right: good breath support, placement, and the inner smile are the key elements here. Don't sustain "dance" if you feel any strain at all. If you're not sure, shake your head "no" as you hold the note to release any throat tension.

If you can comfortably sustain "dance", try several ways to end the note:

1) End it loud by simply stopping the air flow after you articulate the "-nce" of "dance."

2) Try fading to a softer volume, keeping your support muscles active throughout. If you're in chest voice you may move into a mix or head register as the volume lessens.

3) Try adding vibrato. If you are comfortable with your vibrato you may be able to do this at will. If not, try slowly closing your mouth as you sustain the vowel. This can weaken your hold on the note and a vibrato may slip in. One of the beautiful things about diphthong vowels is that you can let a vibrato in as you close to the smaller vowel. It's a technique you'll hear a lot in jazz.

Expansion Ideas

If you listen to the original version of "I Hope You Dance," you'll hear Lee Ann Womack use many of stylizing ideas I've discussed so far, such as passing tones, appoggiaturas, and phrasing. When you've got the song down, experiment with adding those as well as other ornaments like neighboring tones and alternative notes. Have fun with it and sing perhaps too many variations, then look at the lyric and pare down the style ideas until you have something that sounds both different from the original and completely yours.

Check out Lee Ann Womack's version of "I Hope You Dance."

I Hope You Dance

Mark Sanders & Tia Sellers

I hope you never lose your sense of wonder
You get your fill to eat but always keep that hunger
May you never take one single breath for granted
God forbid love ever leave you empty handed
I hope you still feel small when you stand beside the ocean
Whenever one door closes I hope one more opens
Promise me that you'll give faith a fighting chance
And when you get the choice to sit it out or dance

I hope you dance
I hope you dance

I hope you never fear those mountains in the distance
Never settle for the path of least resistance
Livin' might mean takin' chances but they're worth takin'
Lovin' might be a mistake but it's worth makin'
Don't let some hell bent heart leave you bitter
When you come close to sellin' out—reconsider
Give the heavens above more than just a passing glance
And when you get the choice to sit it out or dance

I hope you dance
I hope you dance
I hope you dance
I hope you dance

Bridge Over Troubled Water

Focus: Putting It All Together
Sound: Your Choice
Alto/Bass Key: Ab
Baritone/Soprano Key: Db

In "Bridge Over Troubled Water" you'll be synchronizing everything that you've worked on during the workout. Each song until now has had a different focus, and now you can check to see that everything is coordinating smoothly: support, resonance, the works. Singers who want to work on belting can do that with the song after this one. Since belting is one of the most aggressive ways to vocalize you'll want to make sure your technique is down before attempting it.

Putting It All Together with "Bridge Over Troubled Water"

• Sing the song with any sound that you've liked as you've sung the workout. "Nah," "yah," "yeah," or "wo" are all good possibilities. Sing at a medium to medium loud volume. As you sing, go through this checklist:

1. Inhalation: Does it feel relaxed and full? Do you feel expansion in your belly and/or sides? Are your shoulders down?
2. Exhalation: Is your rib cage lifted? Are your support muscles active?
3. Posture: Is your nose pointed straight ahead, neither up nor down?
4. Throat: Is it relaxed? Is your larynx in a neutral position or close to it?
5. Resonance: Do you feel vibration around your eyes, nose and/or mouth?
6. Jaw: Are you dropping it enough on the high notes?
7. Diction (Lyric only): Are you pronouncing the vowels in the easiest way?
8. The inner smile: Can you feel the upper half of your face opening and lifting? Can you arc the sound out through the space the lifting creates?
9. Elasticity: Are your highs as relaxed as possible and your lows controlled and placed?
10. Intonation: Are you in tune?
11. Articulation: Are your consonants light and crisp?

Ultimately, these elements should be automatic so that you can focus on singing the lyrics with feeling.

• When all systems are "go" you can switch to the lyric and go back down the checklist.

Troubleshooting

The low notes in the verses shouldn't be a problem if you sing softly enough and maintain facial resonance. In fact, the start of each verse is a good time to relax, breathe deeply and psych yourself up for the high notes to come. The word "friends" in the first verse take a sudden leap that can surprise you after the ease of the first few phrases. "Pain" and "sailing" fall on the same note in the second and third verses, respectively. For all three, anticipating the leap and shaping "eh" with your mouth can help open and relax the note.

Some other diphthongs to watch for and open are:
"A-round" (shape "ah") just before the first chorus.
"A-bout" (shape "ah") just before the second chorus.
"Be-hind" (shape "ah") just before the last chorus.
"Like" (shape "ah") in every "like a bridge over troubled water."
"Mind" (shape "ah") at the end of the song. You can see that though there are lots of high notes in the chorus, most of them have a nice open "ah" vowel in them.

Lighten up on the L in "troubled." Sustain an "ou" vowel (as in "bull") on that second syllable.

The last time the word "bridge" occurs is on a killer high note. Open the "ih" vowel almost to "eh," and keep the inner smile.

Another difficulty with "Bridge Over Troubled Water" is its length. I've had several students who sang it fine technically but ran out of steam on the third verse. If you feel your strength ebbing you have a couple of options. You can hit the pause button mid-song and take a breather, then pick up where you started. Or, you might just sing the first verse for a week before adding the second verse, then a week later add the third. This will give you time to build stamina. As always, don't plow on if your voice is tired. Not only will this strain your voice, but you could psychologically start assuming that you'll strain every subsequent time you sing the song. Going slowly is a better plan for success.

Expansion Ideas

Though Simon & Garfunkel's original version of "Bridge Over Troubled Water" was sung with almost no ornamentation, I think the song itself has a gospel feel to it. Gospel singers use every stylistic trick in the book, and often sing “runs.” In r&b, blues, and rock you’ll also hear a lot of runs, which are either several ornaments strung together or variations on a pentatonic scale. Altos and basses, in the key of Ab the pentatonic scale is Ab, Cb, Db, Eb, Gb, Ab. Baritones and sopranos, in the key of Db the pentatonic scale is Db, Fb, Gb, Ab, Cb, Db. You can use fragments of this scale to create runs. For instance, in the first verse of "Bridge Over Troubled Water," baritones and soprano can sing the usual Db on the last note of "worry," then glide the word down Cb and Ab, descending down the pentatonic scale. On the next phrase, on the word "small," slide down to Db then do a double neighboring tone, singing Fb, Db, Cb, and Db again. Altos and basses can do the same in their key of Ab. Land on the Ab on the word "weary," then stretch the word down over Gb and Eb. When you sing "small," try adding Ab, Cb, Ab, Gb, and Ab again. All singers can then try a longer descending pentatonic run on “eyes” at the end of the next phrase, then end the phrase after that on a pentatonic run that ascends, then returns. Listen to the style section on CD #2 to hear examples of these ideas.

Another way to play with pentatonic variations is to learn the pentatonic scale that works for a song, then sing passing tones, neighboring tones, etc., using a pentatonic scale instead of the major and minor scales we’ve used so far for these ornaments.

Check out the versions of "Bridge Over Troubled Water" by these artists:

Simon & Garfunkel • Leann Rimes • Aretha Franklin • Clay Aiken

Bridge Over Trouble Water

Paul Simon

When you're weary, feeling small
When tears are in your eyes
I'll dry them all
I'm on your side--oh, when times get rough
And friends just can't be found
Like a bridge over troubled water
I will lay me down
Like a bridge over troubled water
I will lay me down

When you're down and out
When you're on the street
When evening falls so hard I will comfort you
I'll take your part—oh, when darkness comes
And pain is all around
Like a bridge over troubled water
I will lay me down
Like a bridge over troubled water
I will lay me down

Sail on silver girl
Sail on by
Your time has come to shine
All your dreams are on their way
See how they shine
If you need a friend
I'm sailing right behind

Like a bridge over troubled water
I will ease your mind
Like a bridge over troubled water
I will ease your mind

Cry

Focus: Belting
Sound: Yeah, Yah, Nah
Alto/Bass Key: Gb/G/Ab
Baritone/Soprano Key: B/C/Db

Turn on your radio and you'll hear a lot of belting going on in every contemporary vocal style. Belting is a loud, full-voiced sound that occurs when the chest voice is carried past the point where the voice would normally shift to a mix or head register. When done incorrectly it can be very hard on the voice, so on your behalf I'm going to now be a little paranoid. It's very easy to strain when you're doing belt work, so please obsessively monitor yourself for any signs of strain. Back off if you feel any vocal fatigue: either skip "Cry" until you've built up more strength, or work on it with a teacher. Developing a belt without a teacher standing there assisting you can be tricky work, but since belting is such a common vocal style I think it's important to address it here.

Most singers can build up enough vocal strength and support to carry one's chest voice past its usual transition point. But at some point in your range you may feel you've hit a wall. In fact, pushing your chest voice higher can increase the break in-between registers. Some vocal styles, like traditional country, use that break for effect. There can be a vulnerable feeling conveyed when your voice suddenly switches to a lighter register. However, many singers simply want the option of sounding as strong as possible on their high notes. I think the ideal way is to develop a modified belt that is part mix, part belt. The tone is still strong but you won't feel like you're yelling. Steve Perry's, Barbra Streisand's and Celine Dion's high notes are good examples of a modified belt.

A quick aside here: singers who want to build their belting abilities probably should not try to belt the entire vocal workout. Use the workout up to now as a preparation for belting. If possible, use your mix register on high notes throughout the workout. Mixed notes will prepare you better for belting than singing in a head voice. That being said, sopranos may need to move into head register on some of the workout's higher notes. Baritones, basses, and altos may be able to stay in chest or mix register throughout. I'd also recommend working with the rest of the workout for at least a couple of months before tackling "Cry," unless you are an advanced singer.

Gently rest your fingers on your larynx as you do this work. When belting correctly you may feel the larynx tip forward. What you *don't* want to feel is that the larynx is moving higher in your throat.

The work you do here is similar to volume work: make sure that you have enough breath support, then arc the sound out through your eyes as you maintain the inner smile. Try exclaiming "yeah!" as you did before, but each time start on a slightly higher note. Do this at a loud volume. If you have a piano and know your notes, play an Ab as your starting note (a bit higher if you are a baritone or soprano), then move up in half-steps. Each "yeah!" should resonate a little higher in your head. If you feel like you hit a wall, try using "nyeah" instead—the extra nasality could bring in more mix to modify the belt. If this doesn't feel good at all don't push it.

What you're doing here is encouraging the vocal cords to carry a chestier tone higher without making them sustain the note. You also might be blending some of your mix register in with your chest sound. If these higher notes feel strong you can try the same sequence of "yeahs," but this time hold the first note a bit longer. Next, try the same sequence with "yah," or "nah." Keep monitoring your throat for any signs of fatigue. Also watch that your chin doesn't tip up and that you keep your nose pointed straight ahead.

Belting "Cry"

For those of you familiar with the Faith HIll version, the alto/bass version starts a whole step lower than hers, and in the final chorus modulates up to her key.

• Sing the song on "yeah," "yah," "nah," whichever you have found to be easiest during the workout. This is the rangiest song of the workout, so it's possible the highest or lowest notes will be beyond your range. On the low parts of the verse you can practically hum it with "nouh" or "youh" (rhymes with could) if that helps to place the notes. When you get to each chorus, if you want to try belting, at first sing the high notes with quick, unsustained "yeahs," "yahs," or "nahs." You can sustain them longer if they feel comfortable or if you are singing them in mix or head register.

• Sing the lyric as if you were drunk to keep your throat relaxed. Slide around the high notes.

• Sing the lyric with normal enunciation. Since the second half of the song modulates higher, you might want to work the first half of the song until you've mastered it, then work on the second half.

Troubleshooting

The word "something" in the chorus falls on the highest note of the workout and you probably won't be able to belt it: mix it or do it in head voice. This note is higher than the standard bass, alto, soprano or baritone range high note, so don't worry if it's still too high for you. Just substitute the note you sing on the word "cry."

Whether you are singing with the sounds or the lyric, try all of these methods to help you belt the rest of the song safely—they also will help if you are in mix or head register and having difficulty getting to the high notes:

• Slowly shake your head "no" as you sing.
• Drop your jaw more on high notes.
• Imagine that you are singing out, not up, on high notes. One way to do this is to pitch an imaginary ball overhand as you sing a high note like the one on "cry".
• Maintain the inner smile.
• Remember that the higher you sing, the higher you should feel the resonance in your head.

If nothing works, skip the high notes for now or sing in a mix or head register. Remember, strengthening the vocal muscle is not like working your biceps at the gym.

You don't want to "go for the burn" or think that you gave them a real good workout because your throat feels tired. What you might feel after singing a hard song like "Cry" is that your entire body is pooped. That's usually a good sign; it means that you are using your entire body to support your singing. Belting should feel like it takes extra effort, but never strain.

The words "cry," "lie," and "die" all fall on very high notes. Go for the "ah" in the diphthong to open them. If you've ever seen Faith Hill sing this song you'll know that she hyper-extends her jaw to reach the high notes. While you don't want to hyper-extend your jaw as a rule, for extreme high notes like those in "Cry" you may need to.

Downplay the L on "little" in the chorus so you don't swallow the sound. If you sustain the second syllable of "little" focus on an "uh" sound.

The verse melodies include the lowest notes of the workout. If singing them at a soft volume with your mouth fairly closed doesn't facially place them, substitute some higher notes.

Expansion Ideas

Since "Cry" is a technical workout, skip ornaments on it and just focus on good singing.

Check out versions of "Cry" by these singers:

Faith Hill • Angie Aparo

Cry

Angie Aparo

If I had just one tear running down your cheek
Maybe I could cope, maybe I'd get some sleep
If I had just one moment at your expense
Maybe all my misery would be well spent

Could you cry a little?
Lie just a little?
Pretend that you're feeling a little more pain?
I gave, now I'm wanting
Something in return
So cry just a little for me

If your love could be caged
Honey, I would hold the key
And conceal it underneath the pile of lies you handed me

And you'd hunt those lies
They'd be all you'd ever find
And that'd be all you'd have to know
For me to be fine

And you'd cry a little
Die just a little
And, baby, I would feel just a little less pain
I gave, now I'm wanting
Something in return
So cry just a little for me

Give it up, baby
I hear you're doing fine
Nothin's gonna save me
I see it in your eyes
Some kind of heartache comin'
Give it a try
I don't want pity
I just want what is mine—yeah

Could you cry a little?
Lie just a little?
Pretend that you're feeling a little more pain
I gave, now I'm wanting
Something in return
So cry just a little for me

Cry a little
Lie just a little?
Pretend that you're feeling a little more pain
I gave, now I'm wanting
Something in return
So cry just a little for me
Cry just a little for me

Song Study Order

Here are some areas to cover as you work on a song, in the order I usually use. The last few areas influence each other so there's no crucial order. Remember to check back with earlier items as you move along—it's easy, for example, to get wrapped up in style and forget about breathing.

1. Notes: Learn the notes as written before adding any variations.
2. Rhythm: Learn the rhythm as written before adding any variations.
3. Breathing: Note where you're going to breathe on difficult phrases, and note high or long passages where you'll want to support your voice with enough air.
4. Placement: Make sure you feel all notes resonating somewhere in your head, not your throat.
5. Vowel Awareness: Pronounce vowels correctly. This makes singing easier and better sounding.
6. Intonation: Make sure all notes are on the true pitch, neither flat nor sharp.
7. Tone: Is your tone right for the style of the song? Should it be clear, breathy, warm, edgy, or what?
8. Attitude/Emotion: What are you saying with the lyric? Without an emotional element your song will be soulless. I would rather hear an untrained singer who captures the feel of the song than a technically gifted singer who lacks emotion. Note if the emotion changes as the song progresses.
9. Stylizing: Experiment with phrasing, runs, and dynamics. These are different tools to make the song your own and to put it across effectively.
10. Visuals and Stage Presence: Does the rest of your body reflect what your voice is now putting across?

<u>Some Ideas For Working on a Song</u>

- Work with a lyric sheet even if you have it memorized. You can put in breath marks, pronunciation notes, dynamic markings, and emotional cues.
- Mark troublesome passages and concentrate on just those passages the next time you work on the song, before singing the entire song.
- Record yourself and analyze the results using the song study list.
- Jot down the main hurdles or reminders about the song, and scan them before singing the whole thing. Many singers will sing half the song before they remember what they'd figured out the day before.
- If you have several songs worked out to a performance or near-performance level, alternate between them so you have to approach each one fresh—you won't get to repeat a song on stage.

Glossary

• Diaphragm: the muscle that works your lungs when you breathe.

• Diphthong: a combination vowel comprised of two simple vowels, an open vowel followed by a closed vowel. The mouth must move to pronounce it.

• Glottal Attack: a grabbing of the vocal cords that sometimes occurs when singing a word that begins with a vowel. Glottal attacks tire the voice.

• Inner Smile: a facial position where the soft palate is lifted and the sinuses are open. The upper half of the face feels open and lifted.

• Larynx: the voice box in the throat where the vocal cords are found.

• Looping: carrying the last consonant in a word over to the next word to maximize time on the vowel and make one's singing more flowing.

• Melisma: a vowel sound that is carried over several notes. Runs are also melismas.

• Ornamentation: a one- to four-note addition to a note. Here are the basic ornamentations, written in numeric form, e.g.: in the key of C: C=1, D=2, E=3, F=4, G=5, A=6, B=7, C=8:

Neighboring tone: a step away in either direction, then a return to the first note. 121, 565, 878, 323, etc.

Appoggiatura: singing one step above the desired note, then resolving down. 43, 21, 65, etc. Less common are upward resolving appoggiaturas, usually sung in the blues.

Passing tone: A descent or ascent from the note in stepwise motion to the next note that fits the chord. This will always be two or three steps away.
321, 543, 5678, 345.

Throb: a double attack on a note, using a surge of air. 88, 33, 11 etc.

Alternate chordal note: A jump of a third or a fourth to the nearest note that also belongs in the chord being played. One can sing the melody note then go to the alternate chordal note, or skip the melody note and go right to the alternate. 31, 135, 853, etc.

I sing examples of most of these ornaments at the end of CD #2.

• Pentatonic Scale: a five note scale based on the natural minor scale. Fragments and variations of the pentatonic scale are often used for runs. Numerically, the notes are: 1 , b3, 4, 5, b7. In the key of A, for example, the pentatonic scale would be A, C, D, E, G.

• Phrasing: singing the same notes of a given melody while altering the rhythm.

• Placement: feeling the voice vibrate in the resonance spots of the head: the mouth, nose, cheekbones, and around the eyes.

• Range: all of the notes a singer can sing.

• Register: different areas of the voice that make up the entire range. Singers are commonly thought to have two or three registers: head and chest; or head, mix, and chest.

• Resonance: the bouncing of vibrating air against different parts of the body, creating the vocal sound. When singing correctly one feels resonance in various parts of the head and sometimes the chest. Though the vibration starts in the throat, too much much throat resonance can lead to vocal fatigue.

• Run: an extended ornamentation added to the melody, also called a riff or fill.

• Scoop: a slide up to a note.

• Simple Vowel: a vowel that can be pronounced with your mouth in one position.

• Soft Palate: the back of the roof of the mouth, directly behind the hard palate. The soft palate lifts when you yawn.

• Vocal Cords: muscle folds, surrounded by tissue and a mucous membrane, through which air passes, causing a vibration that resonates in the body and becomes the voice.

Singer's Tools: Tips From the Road

reprinted from Backstage West

You've had five years of voice training, your technique is solid, and then a cold destroys your sound the day of your big show. Unfortunately, everything that effects your body can also effect your vocal cords, including sickness, stress, diet, the weather, and lack of sleep. I've picked up a lot of tips over the years for dealing with voice problems that aren't caused by improper voice technique, but I thought the real experts here would be touring singer-songwriters. These hardy souls are the ones who sometimes sleep on a friend's floor, then drive six hours through the snow to do another gig in a drafty auditorium during flu season. My contributors are:

Jonatha Brooke • Don Conoscenti (aka Doncon) • Kristina Olsen
Darryl Purpose • Tanya Savory • Eric Schwartz {Add ".com" to their names to reach their websites.}

Since all bodies are different you will need to experiment with these ideas. That being said, there are some general principles that hold true for all voices. Vocal cords like warmth and moisture. When they dry out, your voice may crack or otherwise misbehave. "I drink a LOT of water, constantly," says Darryl Purpose. Don Conoscenti elaborates: "Hydration is key for me. I drink loads of water, no ice...always room temp at least. It's especially important during the hour or two before the show."

How much? "Two to three large Evian bottles," says Jonatha Brooke. Los Angeles voice doctor Carlton Lee recommended a gallon a day to one of my students. Try to avoid ice cubes since cold water can constrict your vocal cords. Sipping hot water or herbal tea is soothing because you are inhaling steam at the same time.

Heaters in the winter and air conditioners in the summer both zap moisture out of the air and dry out your cords. "I hate air conditioning and heaters equally," says Tanya Savory. "I turn everything off at night unless the weather is just hideously hot or cold. I open windows or use extra blankets." If you use the AC or heater in your car, turn the vents to direct the flow away from your face.

Cold air can also tighten your vocal cords and tax your immune system. "If the venue or stage is cold I try to maintain a warm body temperature by wearing a turtleneck, sweater or a hat," says Doncon.

Humidifiers are a dried out singer's best friend. Use the ten dollar kind that just boils water, and remember to clean them to keep them mold-free. A hot shower can also put some moisture back into your vocal cords.

There are numerous throat sprays available that can help a dry throat. Look for soothing ingredients like slippery elm and licorice. Kristina adds: "Dr. Robert Andrews, my voice doctor and Mariah Carey's, told me to not use any lozenges that anesthetize your throat because you don't feel the pain and you can really damage your voice."

Needless to say, smoking not only dries out but also irritates your vocal cords.

Another throat irritant is overuse of the voice. Eric Schwartz says "I try not to yell at my agent on my cellphone if I'm going more than forty miles an hour, the road noise is too much to compete with. Oh, right, I don't have an agent. No wonder my voice is in such good shape!" "No talking in loud bars or in noisy forms of transportion," says Kristina.

Some singers are dramatically affected by diet, for others it's no big deal. "When I first started touring heavily, I was really superstitious about dairy, coffee, sleep, air conditioning etc." says Jonatha. Now I drink plenty of coffee, a ton of water, eat whatever I want, and I'm usually fine."

Other singers have found that it pays to be careful. Eric says "Avoiding alcohol is good 'cuz it's a diuretic and thus dehydrates. Of course so's coffee but tough noogies...I can't sing if I'm asleep!" Another drying substance besides alcohol and coffee is citrus, so avoid lemonade and orange juice an hour or two before singing.

Overly spicy foods and coffee can irritate your throat, so watch out for that chimichanga and latte. Some foods can gunk up your sound. Doncon says: "I maintain a dairy-free diet to eliminate mucous and keep my sinuses clear." Kristina is also careful: " Very little caffeine, very little alcohol, no dairy, no wheat, no sugars." Any foods you are sensitive to (wheat is a common offender) will increase throat crud.

When you eat is important, too. Jonatha confides: "If I eat a big meal right before I sing I end up having to fight burps on any extended notes, and that's really hard and embarrassing!" Try to eat a couple of hours before the show.

Colds and allergies are prime mucous creators and the bane of touring artists, so these singers do a lot of prevention. Darryl Purpose says: "I try to work out, eat well, and sleep till I wake up if I can." Doncon says: "I run most days, do yoga and consume a lot of spirulina. In all my years of touring I have avoided fast food like the plague that it is." Still, Jonatha thinks that colds are inevitable on tour: "Colds are just a reality of being on a big dirty bus with a bunch of dirty people. All you can do is drink a ton of water, inhale vitamin C and echinacea, and really pace yourself during shows."

Controversy reigns about the efficacy of garlic, echinacea and zinc lozenges for cold prevention, but I'm a fan of all three. Kristina has two more tricks: "Mostly my diet keeps me from getting colds, but I do wear an air filter (Air Supply, you can get it from Magellan's travel catalogue) when I am in any crowded space, especially airplanes. It sounds funny but it really seems to work. Also, if I feel a cold coming on I use Zicam, a homeopathic nasal gel that lessens the symptoms."

The healthy diet that many of these singers opt for can build your immune system and help you fight allergies as well. Doncon says: "You'd be surprised how healthy you get when you exercise regularly and stop eating dairy products and refined foods." If you do choose to medicate for your allergies, avoid oral antihistamines like Sudaphed which can also overly dry your vocal cords as they dry up your nose. Some voice doctors recommend that allergic singers use a nasal spray like Nasalchrom or Flonase and point it up so the spray doesn't hit the back of the nose, drip down and dry out the vocal cords.

A gentle, cheap way to de-gunk your throat is gargling. Kristina favors "Gargling with warm salt water and snorting warm salt water up my nose when it is running like crazy."

If a cold or allergy attack hits you the day of a show? "Rest, lots of hot tea (herbal, if possible,) and extra warming up, especially humming," prescribes Eric. If the cold is really irritating your vocal cords, rest your voice until shortly before your gig. If you must talk, speak in the middle of your range at a low volume. Rehearse your songs without singing, or just rehearse your set mentally. Kristina says "When my voice is out, I do the yoga lion [that's the pose with your tongue stuck way out], tongue rolls and sloppy chews."

If you get the dreaded cold or allergy attack the day of a show, pray for performance anxiety. The stage nerves that you've always hated can deliver a shot of adrenaline, which will knock out most of your symptoms for the duration of the show.

Sick or healthy, touring singers do a lot on the road and pre-performance to prepare their voices. Doncon says: "I do sirens, yoga, vocal stretches, and avoid too much conversation during the hour prior to the gig." Tanya says: "I go for a run of at least 30-40 minutes. It doesn't matter if I have to run around a parking lot somewhere in New Jersey twenty times, the run is going to happen. It relaxes everything. If I'm really tired it re-energizes me...it's way better than a nap." Darryl's pre-performance regimen: "Anything that helps me relax helps my singing. Bathroom yoga, a shoulder rub, a moment or two of quiet time—they all help."

Jonatha has a final sage comment: "Try to get some sleep! I'm not a big party animal and I think that the only way you can sing five or six nights in a row is if you're kind of boring and go to bed as early as possible."

On Singing and Aging

I saw Ella Fitzgerald sing when she was in her fifties and she sounded like a nineteen-year-old. Until failing health caused her to stop singing she sounded pretty much the same as when she was young. Mel Torme also sounded great as he aged. Steven Tyler is well into his fifties and can out-wail most rockers half his age. Stevie Wonder, Natalie Cole, and Elvis Costello are all well past forty and singing better than when they were younger.

All of these singers are my role models for aging. They figured out what they needed to do to keep their voices strong and they did it. Stevie Wonder and Natalie Cole both had vocal problems early in their careers and were forced to learn good voice technique. That may be why they sound so good today. I've read that Tony Bennett still does daily voice exercises. I saw him sing recently and he was singing notes a third higher than his co-bill Diana Krall!

Everything I've already talked about in this book will help your voice stay supple as you age, but here are some other points to remember.

Don't smoke. Duh. Listen to early Rosemary Clooney, then late Rosemary. Ditto Joni Mitchell. Their constant smoking irritated their vocal cords, changed their tone and killed off their high notes. Nothing will age your voice faster than smoking. Well, maybe drinking.

Rosemary Clooney also acquired a vibrato you can drive a car through as she aged. (My apologies to Ms. Clooney and Ms. Mitchell for picking on them.) It's very easy to lose muscle strength as we age. One place this shows up in aging singers is in the low end: low notes become hard to control and are replaced by a gigantic wobble. To combat this, make sure to sing low songs or exercises daily with no vibrato. The sound may be too buzzy or controlled for your taste, but do it anyway to keep your vocal cords toned. Remember that "ee" is the easiest vowel to control on low notes, so try songs on "dee," "lee," or "mee."

Singers that rely a great deal on their head register (or falsetto) often find their highs grow weak as they get older. Judy Davis (Barbra Streisand's coach) told me that this part of the vocal apparatus is the first to weaken with age. Developing a strong mix register will give you continued strong high notes. Ella Fitzgerald always sang her highs in a mix, which is one reason her voice didn't age as her body did.

Staying in good physical condition is a big help. It's hard work to sing correctly. Your entire body has to work to support and keep the vocal cords from overworking. Mick Jagger at sixty+ is in better shape than many singers half his age. That helps him get through his energetic shows, and it keeps his voice strong. Weight-bearing exercises like hiking and weightlifting build strong bones and muscles. Yoga is great for posture and breathing, and many yoga postures are also good weight-bearing exercises. Swimming is excellent for increasing lung capacity while being easy on creaky knees.

The lack of estrogen in post-menopausal women can cause voices to get drier and crackly. Breath support and correct placement will help this. Drink plenty of water to keep the cords hydrated. Read "Singer's Tools" for more ideas about battling dryness.

Voices can last a lot longer than we think. Last summer I was talking to Velzoe Brown, a then 89-year-old singer and musician who still performs regularly with her band. She complained to me that her voice had gone crackly and I asked when that had happened. "Oh, six years ago." she said. That means her voice was fine until she turned 83. We should all be so lucky!

About the Author

Susan Anders, MA, has coached singers for over twenty-five years. Her students include major and independent label recording artists and TV and film actors. Susan's articles on singing have appeared in *Acoustic Guitar*, *Acoustic Musician* and *Backstage West/Dramalogue*. Her singing methods include *Harmony Singing by Ear*, *Singing with Style*, and *Singing Live*. She has recorded five albums with her former band Susan's Room, as well as a solo album and a lullaby album. Currently she is working on a second solo album and a vocal warm-up for kids. Susan was born and raised in Berkeley, California, and now lives in Nashville, Tennessee. More information on Susan is available at www.susananders.com.

Produced and Engineered by Tom Manche at Studio X in Nashville, Tennessee

The Band
Vocals: Susan Anders
Vocals: Perry White
Guitars: Tom Manche
Keyboards: Perry Barton
Bass: Dave Francis
Drums: Bryan Owings

CD Track Lists

CD #1

1) Introduction
2) Clearly Intro
3) I Can See Clearly
4) Prudence Intro
5) Dear Prudence
6) Do Right Intro
7) Why Don't You Do Right?
8) Gotta Be Intro
9) You Gotta Be
10) Summer Intro
11) Summertime
12) One Intro
13) One Of Us
14) Get Here Intro
15) Get Here
16) I'm Beginning Intro
17) I'm Beginning to See the Light
18) Don't Know Intro
19) Don't Know Why
20) Sunday Intro
21) Sunday Kind Of Love
22) Thank You Intro
23) Thank You
24) You're Still Intro
25) You're Still The One
26) Tracks Intro
27) Tracks of My Tears
28) Ms. Celie's Intro
29) Ms Celie's Blues
30) Alison Intro
31) Alison
32) Dance Intro
33) I Hope You Dance
34) Bridge Intro
35) Bridge Over Troubled Water
36) Cry Intro
37) Cry

CD #2

1) I Can See Clearly
2) Dear Prudence
3) Why Don't You Do Right?
4) You Gotta Be
5) Summertime
6) One Of Us
7) Get Here
8) I'm Beginning to See the Light
9) Don't Know Why
10) Sunday Kind Of Love
11) Thank You
12) You're Still The One
13) Tracks of My Tears
14) Ms. Celie's Blues
15) Alison
16) I Hope You Dance
17) Bridge Over Troubled Water
18) Cry
19) Stylizing Examples

52147868R00044

Made in the USA
Lexington, KY
15 September 2019